Rescuing Used Coonhounds

ANN M. JAYNE

Published by BookBaby
7905 North Route 130
Pennsauken, NJ 08110
877-961-6878
www.bookbaby.com

Paperback ISBN: 978-1-09836-6-681
eBook ISBN: 978-1-09836-6-698

Rescue:

To free from confinement, danger, or evil.
Save, Deliver.

Merriam-Webster Dictionary

"GOD" spelled
backwards is "DOG."

This book is dedicated to Casey and Bowie for their love and lessons. It is also dedicated to the people who have rescued, fostered, or adopted any dog, but particularly a Coonhound. I believe God sends these dogs to us and He sends us to these dogs. I know my life changed the day God sent my Coonhounds to me. I'm forever grateful.

Contents

...You rescued me because You delighted in me.

Psalm 18:19

What is a "used" coonhound?

O ne of my favorite movies is *Secondhand Lions*. In this movie, Robert Duvall and Michael Caine play two brothers who try to fend off old age and boredom by purchasing a lion so they can go on "safari." Their great-nephew, played by Haley Joel Ozment, lives with them. When the lion arrives, rather than being a majestic "king of the beasts" from the plains of Africa, she turns out to be a secondhand, used, and "worn-out" lioness. But her purpose is yet to be discovered.

A "used" coonhound is like the lioness in the movie. However, instead of being a work of fiction or creature in someone's imagination, the used coonhounds in my book are real. They've endured unimaginable horrors and abuse, things no animal should ever have to experience. Ever. And yet, here they are with love to give and lessons to teach, waiting to be rescued.

I don't know what sort of monsters owned the dogs, including my Casey and Bowie, whom I will tell you about in this book. But they surely have some similar characteristics:

- starve the dog

- beat the dog

- kick the dog

- abuse the dog

- torture the dog

- shoot the dog with buckshot or BBs

- burn the dog

- tie up the dog with a chain or rope

- keep the dog caged, often with only a wire "floor" for the dog to stand/lay on

- dump out the dog to fend for itself

- deprive the dog of shelter

- deprive the dog of water

- have *ZERO* love and compassion for the dog

- Or be—in one simple, despicable, horrible word—*cruel*.

How can a human being treat *any* animal this way? And yes, kids are included in this, as well. I'm not disregarding child abuse at all. Perhaps if I had taken in an abused child, I would be writing a book about that. But I have rescued a coonhound and subsequently I've been made aware of their plight across the United States.

I got the idea for this book while driving home from teaching one of my yoga classes. I have a "Happiness" playlist of songs that make me happy. One of those songs is "Home" by Phillip Phillips. This song was released in May 2012 and used for the U.S. women's gymnastics team in the 2012 Beijing Summer Olympics. I fell in love with the song immediately. It is special to me because I relate to it as God talking to me about getting through this life.

Troubles come, but I have a home in heaven. At the particular time that I was listening to this song, I wasn't thinking about our talented gymnasts bouncing around. I was thinking about how God rescues us. And then I started thinking about Casey and other coonhounds. I began to really listen to the words of this song.

Then I started to cry.

This song is fitting for any rescued animal who has been the victim of abuse. Horses are my other love and seem especially susceptible to starvation, neglect and cruelty, because some people are stupid. And mean. I truly believe there is a very, very, very special place in hell reserved for people who abuse and torture children and animals.

Abused animals (and humans) are lifted up in my prayers. I ask God to let someone find them and love them and give them a home, to *rescue* them. I pray that they find out what love and kindness are.

In this book, I have included some scriptures. In no way am I trying to change the meaning of the Bible or what God says. Jesus Christ is our Savior. Amen. But some of the scriptures, I believe, are appropriate. God wants us to be kind and love one another. I believe He means for us to love and be kind to His creatures as well. And while some scripture specifically speaks about God's love for us, I think it can include His love, and ours, for our coonhounds. So please don't take this in any other way than that I simply believe that we are to be good stewards and take care of these animals God sends to us.

In my little book, I am going to tell you about some of these angels God has sent to rescue His sweet, soulful coonhounds. They need these people. And as I have found out, we need these coonhounds. Who rescues whom?

Chapter 1

It Started with Beagles

Beagle: One of the world's most recognizable hounds and dogs, the Beagle is essentially a small foxhound, solid and "big for his inches." (1)

As far back as I can remember, I have loved dogs and horses. We had a collie named Lady when I was very little. I don't remember her at all, but I'm sure I loved her. Many dogs have come and gone in my life, and you will get to read snippets of their lives.

My love affair with dogs, particularly beagles, was fueled by my great-grandfather, Franklin Martin Casey. "F.M." or "Mart" was my mother's maternal grandfather. He was born April 9, 1887 and passed away March 4, 1977.

Grandpa Casey was known as "The Beagle Man." He had beagles and hunting dogs all of his life. Grandpa Casey had a third-grade education, and yet, on every photograph (he loved having his picture taken) he would write the date, place and people in the photo. On photos, paper where he had written notes, and in his Bible, he would draw a beagle's head.

There were 13 kids in Grandpa Casey's family. He was born in Missouri several years after the Civil War ended and lived in the country. Out in the sticks. In the boondocks. Hunting was not only a way of life; it was how he and his family ate. Grandpa Casey (strong Irish descent) and his wife, Eula (strong German descent), had five kids: four boys and my grandmother, Opal ("Meme"). All of the kids' names began with O: Otis, Orlon, Oscar, Opal and Olen, who died about the age of two.

I remember, when I was about the age of five, going out with Grandpa Casey into the country to get some beagle puppies. I believe he named these puppies Mutt and Jeff. My sister Jennifer remembers watching Grandpa Casey gently catch hummingbirds in his hands. He could also get the neighborhood squirrels to eat nuts and crackers out of his hands. He just seemed to have a way with animals, and he always had animals around him.

Meme's brother, Oscar, lived in the country. I loved going to his farm to ride horses, play with his border collie, and gather eggs or pick blackberries. My other sister, Valerie, the oldest, remembers watching in horror as Meme caught chickens at Oscar's farm and wrung their necks! I missed that little life experience. My memories involved galloping around on Sugar, Oscar's gray and white Welsh pony.

I didn't ever know my great-grandmother, Eula. She died way before I was born. But Grandpa Casey remarried, and he and Mary, his second wife lived in a little house on the east side of Okemah, Oklahoma, where I grew up. I remember going there and looking at the gourds that grew on the north and east side of their house. They also had a little concrete slab that served as a "bridge" over a small ditch on the west side of their house. What fascinated me was that multi-colored marbles had been placed into the wet cement. I'm not sure, but I think "Casey" was spelled out with the marbles.

Mary died and Grandpa Casey moved from their house to a little apartment on the north side of Okemah. Later he moved to a little house behind Meme and her husband, Grandpa George, on the south side of Okemah, on Seventh Street. He only lived a block from me, so I would sprint up the alley to see him.

One day, to my delight, he had two beagle puppies, Sue and Screamer. I would visit him, and we would sit on his little front porch, with the beagles, and swat flies with his fly swatter.

Grandpa Casey began having minor heart "spells" and needed to move to the nursing home. But up until he moved into the Pioneer Nursing Home in Okemah, he had his beagles. He found homes for his dogs before he made the transition to the nursing home.

Even though he didn't have beagles, Grandpa Casey loved living in the nursing home. He used Grecian Formula on his hair so he wouldn't look old (he was in his very late 80s). He used it only on the front of his hair, as his arms were getting too stiff to put it on the back of his head, so the hair there was gray. He had a girlfriend, Caldonia, and also kept a list of the crazy people. He loved riding in Valerie's little red Volkswagen Beetle. Red was his favorite color.

Grandpa Casey was a snappy dresser, too. He loved wearing ties and brightly-colored shirts. The one that stands out in my mind is a purple shirt, a *very* purple shirt. Pimp purple. Most men, especially men who had grown up in the country, would have died before wearing a purple shirt! But not Grandpa Casey. He always wore a hat with a brim and a little feather.

In 1977, Grandpa Casey died at the ripe old age of 89. I missed him terribly. I would still love to sit down and talk to him, get some beagles, and swat some flies.

With sincere thanks to Grandpa Casey, when I was around six years old, I remember going to Okmulgee, Oklahoma, with my parents and sisters, and getting a beagle puppy of our very own. The puppies were in a large grassy yard with a wire fence. They ran up and down the fence with us, and we settled on our puppy, whom we named Snoopy.

Snoopy was the perfect dog, and everyone in the family loved him. Well, Mama tolerated him. She has never been an animal person, so obviously I didn't get the dog gene from her. I also didn't get the cleaning/housework gene from Mama either.

Daddy traveled a lot with his work. He was a mechanic on large gas compressors, and he would have to travel to Montana or Wyoming or Canada and work on engines. He was gone for weeks at a time. But, oh when he came home! Daddy had a big work truck, and Snoopy would always run out to greet him and race him to the driveway. Daddy always slowed down so Snoopy could win. Snoopy was so excited to see Daddy, whether it was every night or when Daddy had been gone for a while. Squeaks, whines, wiggles, and barking with sheer joy are how Snoopy greeted Daddy when he stepped out of his truck. The Royal Hound Homecoming if you will.

Daddy loved to grill meat. And you can bet that Snoopy was certainly his constant companion and best friend while he grilled. As always, bits of fat and meat made their way to the ground for Snoopy to gobble up. If the meat was too hot, Snoopy pawed and barked at it until he could eat it.

Daddy took Snoopy rabbit hunting. Once. When he fired his gun, Snoopy headed for the pick-up and never looked back. And he never went hunting again.

Other than the hunting incident, Snoopy loved to ride in Daddy's old pick-up truck. Usually the trips were to the veterinarian, Dr. C.C. Tolleson. His clinic was about three miles east of town. Snoopy hopped up in the truck, put his feet on the dash board, and surveyed everything as he passed it. Until Daddy turned into the vet's driveway. Snoopy must have been able to smell the vet's office because his countenance suddenly changed. He slunk down in the seat and began moping and trying to hide. We had to drag him out of the truck and into the clinic. I can still recall the smell of various medicines that filled my nostrils as I entered the little office.

Snoopy slept under an end table in our den, until it was bedtime. Then Daddy would say, "Okay, Snoopy, it's time for bed." Snoopy had a big box on our screened-in back porch. It had Daddy's army sleeping bag in it. At these dreaded words, Snoopy would crawl out from under the table, walk as slowly as possible to the door, and then out to his bed.

The porch had a wooden screen door opening to the steps, which Snoopy could push open and go out when he needed to. And come in. Snoopy perfected opening the door (with the scratch marks to prove it) by pawing it with his foot again and again and again until the door started moving. When it opened just enough, Snoopy would poke his head in and hop through the opening.

The Beagle is sturdy and compact, conveying high quality with no hint of coarseness. (2)

Snoopy raised two litters of kittens in the old box and sleeping bag. The cats and beagle would curl up together at night and go to sleep. Well, they went to sleep when Snoopy decided enough was enough. Their bed backed up to the west wall of our den and there was a window in this wall. We could pop up over the back of the couch and look at them, listening to the kittens mewing and playing and scuffling around. But when we heard a loud, stern "WOOF," we knew Snoopy was ready to go to sleep. Monkey-business and playing in the big box came to a screeching halt. It was really quiet after that.

On the north side of our house were four hackberry trees. Every fall we would rake the leaves and jump in the pile. On crisp fall nights, Snoopy, the cats, and the neighborhood dogs would sleep in the big pile of leaves. No one kept their dogs penned up, and no one had fenced yards. This was the late 1960s and early 1970s in Okemah, Oklahoma. We could look out the window on our stairway landing and see all sorts of canines and felines curled up in little warm balls in the leaves.

We had Snoopy about eight years. I can't remember exactly how it happened, but Snoopy broke his tail to the point where it had to be amputated. We left him at the vet overnight and during the night, he whacked his tail on something, the wound opened up, and my sweet little Snoopy bled out and passed away. We were absolutely heartbroken. He was such a grand little dog and the perfect pet. I think maybe Daddy took it the hardest. Now there was no one to race home and, even worse, no ecstatic greeting from a little tri-colored beagle. No beagle to bark at him while he grilled meat and "accidentally" dropped bits and pieces of meat. Snoopy left a hole in our hearts. A hole that only dogs can leave. A hole that only dogs can fill.

Before Grandpa Casey died, around 1974, my absolute love for hounds was further tattooed on my heart and soul with the introductions to foxhounds owned by Leroy Lambeth.

Leroy lived a few blocks away from me, on Tenth Street, which was basically at the edge of town. I became fast friends with Leroy, and his hounds, when I went to his barn to ride his horses. His five acres were just like a piece of heaven to me. There were horses *and* dogs! What more could a girl ask for? Leroy became like a grandfather to me.

Leroy used his foxhounds to hunt "wolves" (coyotes) and had a cage in the back of his old green pick-up truck where the hounds would ride on their way to hunt. (He also used that old green pickup to round up any kids in Okemah that would go, and take them to church and Vacation Bible School at the First Baptist Church.)

Princess the foxhound was Leroy's pride and joy. She was also one of the sweetest dogs I have ever known.

American Foxhound: This long-eared hound is sufficiently tall and lightly boned for a hound. ... Independent and

willful, the American Foxhounds excel in pack hunting and yet maintain their individual personalities. Their cheerful tail-wagging way can also be competition-oriented. (3)

On very quiet nights, as I lay in my bed upstairs with the windows open, I could hear Leroy's pack of foxhounds baying and howling. It was a beautiful sound to hear as I drifted off to sleep.

Besides riding his horses, I also enjoyed having Leroy show me his photo albums. His wife, Lela, always had cookies baking, which she would share with me while we looked at photographs.

Many years ago, way before I was born, Leroy had a bald-faced horse named Ball, whom his daughters rode all over the place. And when they rode Ball past a local diner, Ball wouldn't go any further until they stopped and went in and got him an ice cream cone! I loved hearing that story and seeing the photos of Ball. In some of the photos, Leroy had a pet fox. There were lots of photos of horses and dogs.

Leroy was a World War II veteran who fought in Europe and North Africa. Leroy showed me photos from his tour of duty in Europe, particularly the photos of Anzio, Italy. There he found a black mare and rescued her. She was probably his link to his Oklahoma ranch life. I'm sure her farm had been bombed. But Leroy took care of her until they left. Lela told me that Leroy never talked to her about the war, but every now and then, he and his buddies would get together and talk about their experiences. He was at D-Day. I can't imagine the horrors he saw. Thank God for that mare on the beach.

There was a big old barn on Leroy's five acres. When he was younger, Leroy held square dances in the loft of his barn. There was also a pond and I would ride his Welsh pony, Lucky, into the pond, behind the pond on the dam, and all over the five acres. In fact, any horse Leroy owned or who stayed at his barn was ridden by me. And after my parents moved to Oklahoma City (the summer after I graduated from high school in 1980), I bought my first horse, Rowdy, and kept him at Leroy's.

To this day, I dream about that magical place and now Harry, my horse, is the horse who lives there. I would love to be the owner of that piece of my past. And I can't wait to see Grandpa Casey and Leroy again.

Chapter 2

My Dogs Through the Years

For dogs have surrounded me...

Psalm 22:16a

When I was a freshman in junior high, we had a graduation ceremony before we started high school. For my graduation gift, Valerie and her husband, Brett, got me a half-border collie puppy. I named him Charlie, and he followed me everywhere. My favorite memory of him was when I was lying in the floor watching a particularly sad episode of *All My Children*, a top soap opera at that time. Jennifer heard him coming, banging his plastic Cool Whip supper dish. He trotted silently up behind me and put the bowl right on my head. Jennifer burst out laughing, and I did too. And I got Charlie something to eat.

It was summer time, and we went on vacation, so I left Charlie with Leroy. Charlie learned that when Leroy told him to stop barking, he'd better stop. Well, he learned after Leroy told him to stop, and he persisted, so Leroy threw a bucket of water on him. There were no problems with barking after that!

That summer I went to spend a few days with Valerie and Brett in Edmond, OK. Charlie was so glad to see me when I got home! He wouldn't leave my side. Mama and Daddy told me he didn't eat while I was gone.

As I said earlier, no one kept their dogs in fenced yards. One evening when I called Charlie for supper, he didn't show up. He was gone. When Saturday morning rolled around, Daddy went to the animal control station to see if they had picked up Charlie. They had. He had been hit and killed by a car. Daddy broke the news to me, and he was so upset telling me that we both cried. My sweet Charlie was gone.

Losing Charlie really took a toll on me. I'd only had him a few months, but was crazy about this dog. I was very upset and our neighbor, Dale Stovall, noticed it. A few days later he drove home from work, and I waved to him. He told me to come over to the pickup. I did, and he handed me something. I thought it was a kitten because it was so small. It was a puppy! Dale was an insurance salesman, and someone came into his office and told him about the puppy. He called Mama and Daddy to see if he could give me a puppy, and they agreed.

So that is how I got Festus. Festus looked like some sort of spaniel mix, maybe with beagle or dachshund. He had long black and tan hair and fluffy spaniel ears. And although he was small, he could wreak havoc on the house. Jennifer and I left him in the bathroom while we went to school. We came home at lunch and he had managed to open the bathroom door (after he chewed off some wallpaper) and proceeded to uproot our houseplants and chew up newspapers!

Festus had a little bell on his collar and every morning we heard him run up the stairs. He ran into my room and jumped up in my bed. He was quite the jumper; we would set up jumps in the house, throw his ball, and he would bound over them like an Olympic showjumper. We had a floor furnace between the living room and kitchen, and he could sail over that like a deer.

About a year later, he disappeared, along with some other small dogs in the neighborhood. The rumor going around was that someone had come through, stolen our dogs and sold them to laboratories. I was heartbroken. I wrote letters to laboratories begging them to tell me if they had Festus. I also wrote to my congressmen to see if they could try and stop animal testing, but got the same, tired, standard letter their staff responded with for any complaint. I instantly became an opponent of animal testing as well as about 95% of politicians.

I realize, now that Daddy has passed away from colon cancer and I have a son with Type 1 Diabetes, that there needs to be some controlled testing for new drugs and cures. Many of the drugs can also be used to help animals. I do not want the animals to suffer and I pray for a cure for diabetes and cancer. But I absolutely cannot condone testing shaving cream, makeup, shampoo, cleaning products or other toxic household items or toiletries/cosmetics on animals. They basically have the same ingredients in them, so once we know what is harmful and at what amounts, there is absolutely no need to test these products on animals.

So with no chance of ever getting my little Festus back, I bought a dog breed book and began researching what kind of dog I wanted. Since I didn't remember Lady, our collie, I thought it would be great to have a collie. After all, who doesn't love Lassie?

> **This breed is mild-tempered and tolerant of other dogs and pets. It is highly responsive to training and makes an affectionate and protective companion. However, the people-loving Collie readily accepts visitors to the home and therefore does not make a good guard dog. (4)**

I began scouring the newspaper ads for collie puppies and found some for sale. They were $50. In 1977, that was a huge sum of money to pay for a dog. But I had been saving my money, and I called the woman who had the puppies. We agreed to meet in the nearby town of Shawnee, and as she only had females left, she would bring me a female puppy. Daddy and Mama drove me to Shawnee, and the woman never showed up. I cried all the way home.

When we got home, Mama called this woman and chewed her out. If anyone reading this knows my mother, you know what that entails. Needless to say, she agreed to meet us again, and this time she brought my precious collie puppy. I named her Rusty, even though everyone told me that was a boy's name. I didn't care.

Rusty was sable and white, and I thought she was the most beautiful dog in the world. Daddy made a pen for her, and she stayed in it at night. We went on walks and when my parents moved to Oklahoma City in 1980 after I graduated from high school, I would bring her with me when I came back to Okemah to visit. When I got my first horse, Rowdy, she would follow us on our rides.

Rusty would get up on the outdoor lounger with me. There really wasn't enough room, but it didn't stop her. I loved it. If you left food on the table, she would use her long nose to get it, after she looked around to make sure no one was watching!

When I married David Jayne in 1986, Rusty naturally came to live with us. We got Bridgette, our Basset hound puppy, for each other as our wedding gift. Rusty became Bridgette's mother. She gave her a bath every day and paid particular attention to licking inside Bridgette's long, floppy ears.

Rusty was the first dog I ever had who was deathly afraid of storms. She would hear thunder barely rumble, and would be at the back door, scratching to get in. Once we let her in the house or garage, she was fine. On one occasion, when we were at work, she was so terrified that she pulled the screen door off our sliding patio doors. There were scratch marks about 6 feet high on the glass doors where she had tried to get in when a storm blew up. Bridgette was never afraid of storms, but she knew she got to come inside and never seemed to mind that!

I'd never had a Basset hound before. David grew up with one, Cleo. One of David's medical school friends commented that you just "shellac" a Basset hound and prop them up by your door!

Equally happy by the fireside or in the field, the Basset Hound was bred by French monks to hunt in heavy cover. Unlike its depictions as a buffoon in some cartoons, this consummate sniffer dog is very intelligent and extremely tenacious. As a family pet, the Basset Hound is placid and affectionate. (5)

Although Bridgette could lie around and sleep with the best of the Basset hounds, she also loved to play, especially after she ate her supper. We fed Rusty and Bridgette out of Tupperware bowls. David had built a wooden deck off the patio as our yard was split level. Bridgette would run and scoot her bowl all over the deck. We could hear it rattling around. She would pick it up and run with it, then drop it and let it bounce around. She'd carry it back to the deck and scoot it around until she got tired. Every night when it was supper time, we had to look for her bowl. It was never in the same place.

If you have never taught a Basset hound to walk on a leash, you are missing out on one of life's true pleasures. Just kidding.

Despite their charm and classic appearance, Bassets can be stubborn and lazy, so proper discipline and regular exercise are imperative. (6)

The first time we ever took Bridgette for a walk, we made it about a block. She began to cough and choke and pant, and then she flopped down on her side by the curb. David looked at me, and I had a panic-stricken look on my face.

"I think we've killed her!" David exclaimed.

We bent down to check her breathing, and David saw her eyes blink. I think he whistled to her, and we turned around to head for home. She bounced up and trotted all the way back home!

Bridgette – 1, Ann and David – 0.

We also discovered that good intentions, such as leaving an old flannel shirt in the yard for her to sleep on, could turn into a hazard of sorts. I can't remember what I was doing, but David came and got me and told me I had to come see this. He was laughing so hard he could barely speak.

David pointed to the patio door and Bridgette was laying there with her head shoved through the sleeve, which was much smaller than her head. The cuff dangled off her head and shook when she moved her head. It looked like a deflated elephant trunk. Her ears couldn't fit through the sleeve, so they were pulled behind her head. I don't really know what possessed her to stick her head through that sleeve. (But now, as an experienced hound mom, I realize there isn't an explanation for it because they are all complete goofballs. I'm certain that much sniffing was involved.) I snapped a quick picture and we cut the sleeve off her head. We never gave her any type of clothing to sleep on or play with again.

In 1991, Rusty was almost 14 years old. Her liver began to fail and became distended. I had to make a hard, hard decision. I worked for some veterinarians, and I brought her to them to be put to sleep. I held onto her and told her how much I loved her as she drifted off to sleep to bound over the Rainbow Bridge and wait for me. I had lost a friend and part of my family.

When I got home, I learned that animals indeed grieve. Bridgette met me at the door, and I just held on to her. She knew Rusty was gone. When I put her outside, Bridgette walked onto the deck and sat down. Then she lifted her head and howled the longest, saddest and most mournful howl I have ever heard. She had never howled like that before, not even with the fire trucks and ambulances she heard. Bridgette was crying. Grieving. In essence, Bridgette had not only lost her best friend, she had lost her mother.

I knew I needed to get another dog. And I wanted another collie. I searched the ads and soon found collie puppies. These puppies were west of Oklahoma City, so David and I drove out there to "look." Yeah right.

There were only two pups left. They were clean and healthy even though the woman who was selling them looked like she really needed the money. She was only asking $50 for them, and they had American Kennel Club (AKC) papers, not that it really mattered. I had AKC papers on Rusty. Bridgette had papers, but the lady we bought her from never gave them to us. We weren't in the dog-breeding business or going to AKC dog shows so registration papers didn't matter to me. I'm *still* not in the dog-breeding business nor do I show dogs at AKC dog shows, so registration papers are irrelevant to me.

I squatted down to see the pups, and one of them jumped up on my back. He was black and white, almost like a border collie. The other one was not too interactive with me. I knew which dog had picked me out.

Never timid or sullen, the ideal Collie is blessed with an expression that is absolutely distinctive to his breed. The ineffable mysticism and perfection of this expression crystallize the essence of the Collie character. (7)

"I'll take this one," I told the woman. I picked up my new pup, handed her the money, and headed to the car.

As we drove home, David asked me what I was going to name the new dog. I looked at him for a second and said rather definitely, "Jake."

"Why 'Jake'?" David asked.

I explained to him that Daddy's nickname for me was Jake. I don't know why, but Daddy always called me Jake. So now I have a Jake.

Jake curled up on my lap. He didn't seem to mind that he had just been separated from his mother and sibling. I think he knew he was going home. He didn't even whine that night.

When we got home, Bridgette's nose was out of joint for a little while, but soon, she and Jake were best friends.

Jake was a very smart dog, and very sweet. He wasn't scared of storms, either, which was nice! He liked to hop up on our patio table and enjoyed spending time with his "Grandy and Pappy" (Mama and Daddy). Their human grandkids called them Grandy and Pappy. My dogs just happened to be their canine grandkids. They kept the dogs at their house when we went on vacation.

Daddy was happy to have a dog around. He got the biggest grin on his face when I told him I had named my collie "Jake." His chest puffed up with pride.

Mama and Daddy had a large planter on their patio that was full of dirt. Jake would dig and dig in that planter while Mama and Daddy watched. Then they would put the dirt back in the planter so he could dig and dig some more! They spoiled their granddogs like they did their grandkids.

On March 31, 1993, Daddy was diagnosed with colon cancer. It spread to his liver, and that was that. Chemo and radiation didn't help. But Daddy hung on for a little over two years.

In early 1995, I became pregnant with our first child. We were in the process of building a new house on five acres. Daddy had been able to come out, and when I showed him the baby's room, he sat in the window sill and looked around. He was absorbing as much as he could, hoping he could hang on until the baby arrived.

While we were building our dream house, a stray dog showed up. He looked like a German Shepherd/Rottweiler or husky mix. He was skinny but wanted to be friendly. Of course, I brought food and water out to him. I named him Slim. Once you name a dog, they are yours. They become family. I had a veterinarian come out and vaccinate him. Slim became part of our family.

Slim stayed at the new house. The construction workers liked him. Tools and things had been disappearing until Slim arrived. Then our soon-to-be white trash neighbor-from-hell (I could write a book about him) complained about Slim. He said Slim had tried to bite him. (Later we would discover that "Trash" the neighbor had sticky fingers, and Slim made it harder to steal from us.) However, we didn't know this at the time. Animal Control told us we would have to keep Slim tied up. I absolutely refuse to keep an animal tied up. Luckily one of the construction workers had fallen in love with Slim and offered to take him. We agreed, reluctantly, because we loved Slim, too.

Slim found a good home in the country, and we got reports on him and how well he was doing. He was loved. That was good. And we didn't have to worry about getting sued by our trashy neighbor, although the automatic paint sprayer mysteriously disappeared the night after Slim left.

By September 1995, Daddy was rapidly losing his battle with cancer. He stayed in bed a lot, too weak to move around.

Valerie got a dachshund puppy she named Milo. She brought Milo up and placed him on Daddy's chest. Daddy cupped the tiny puppy with his hands, hands that were mostly rough from all of his years working outdoors. But they were so gentle with us and little Milo.

In Daddy's last days, I would lie next to him and he would put his hand on my stomach to feel the baby. My pregnancy turned into a race to see if I would have my baby before Daddy died. I lost that race.

On October 9, 1995, Daddy went to heaven. My baby wasn't due for another month. We had moved Daddy to the hospital and were all gathered around him. As he took his very last breath, and we knew that he was being carried to heaven by angels, my baby began jumping like crazy inside me. The baby had never been this active. I will believe with my last breath that the angels let Daddy see my baby, his grandson, on his way to heaven. I'm sure he got to kiss Ian and tell him he loved him.

Mama's birthday was October 16, and I would turn 33 on October 20. Ian was born in an emergency Caesarean-section on October 31. He had a head full of dark brown hair and looked like Daddy. He still does. What a blessing.

Jake and Bridgette had no trouble adapting to a baby in the house. In the spring of 1996, we moved into our new home. Jake and Bridgette loved their new backyard, and they had lots of room to run, although Bridgette was getting older.

As Ian grew, I would take him and the dogs on walks down the lane we lived on. On one walk, a neighbor's black lab ran toward us. Jake positioned himself between the dog and me! He was clearly protecting Ian and me. His pack. His family.

We loved our dream home. However, we did not love our neighbor like the Bible commands.

"Trash" was our new neighbor, and he had about 500 kids. The rumor from the good neighbors was that his wife was a stripper. None of the kids ever had on clothes, and I even saw Mrs. Trash jumping on the trampoline, in the front yard, naked. I was also unfortunate enough to see Trash himself zipping through the front yard naked as well.

Their house was nothing short of a two-story shack. Broken down cars were parked everywhere as was an attractive, broken-down school bus. Their dogs of choice were naturally pit bulls. Because if you steal for a living, are white trash (and an idiot), and operate a meth lab, you need pit bulls. Pit bulls who cornered David in our garage one day. And pit bulls who savagely attacked Jake in our yard in May of 1999. I was pregnant with Justin, our second child.

It was dark and fairly late at night when I found Jake on our back porch, bleeding and chewed to pieces. I looked and looked for Bridgette, fearing the worst. She was in the dog house and I'm sure that is what saved her. I rushed my Jake to the emergency vet and they said they would call me after they worked on him.

Early the next morning, I received a call from the vet. Jake had passed away during the night. My beautiful collie was gone. The vet said they could call an animal cremation company for me, and I agreed. A couple of sad, sad days later, I picked up Jake's remains. I buried him beneath an elm tree just outside the backyard fence.

I have loved every dog I've ever owned. And although I grieve deeply for them when one dies, I always get another dog fairly quickly. It's not that I'm done grieving; it's simply that I love dogs so much I *need* another dog to love.

Chapter 3

Big Dogs and Beagles

With the killer dogs at large (and Animal Control being absolutely ZERO help), I began taking my gun with me to the mailbox as the pit bulls were always loose and running up and down the street.

While I loved collies, my mind turned to protection for my family, especially my young son, Ian, and baby Justin who would arrive in January. I began researching protective breeds of dogs. A friend at church had a Rhodesian Ridgeback, so I read up on them. They will fight lions—so maybe a pit bull wouldn't be a problem!

A friend I used to work with kept Great Pyrenees dogs to guard their sheep and goats. They have been known to fight bears and to protect anything (family, sheep, etc.) with their lives. The more I read about Great Pyrenees (Pyrs), the more I began to shift towards them. Gentle giants. Devoted. Protective.

Though deterring as a guard, he is docile and easygoing as a pet and especially patient with children. Compared to the Pyrs originally employed as guardians, today's dog has been domestically sweetened. He is, however, equally as noble, courageous, beautiful as his forebears. (8)

In August of 1999, I found an ad for some puppies. They were just a few miles away, so David, Ian and I went "to look." You know what that means.

There were three or four puppies left, and the mother was on site. When we started playing with her puppies, she took that as an opportunity for some alone time, so off she went.

I sat down with the puppies, white balls of soft, wiggly fluff. I told Ian we had to let the puppy pick us. One puppy in particular snuggled up in my lap and stayed there while his siblings tumbled around and eventually ran off to find their mama.

Ian was almost four years old, so I told him this puppy had picked us out. Since I was pregnant with Justin, I like to think that the puppy picked him out, too. While the owner was giving the puppy his first set of shots, David asked me what I was going to name him.

I looked at the puppy and said matter-of-factly and almost instantly, "Baloo." Walt Disney's *The Jungle Book* is my absolute, most favorite cartoon of all time. Baloo the bear was one of my favorite characters because he was so loveable and kind. (Shere Khan the tiger was also my other favorite character.) Baloo had AKC papers, so I registered him as "Super Smoocha Baloo."

Bridgette was less-than-thrilled at first, but soon she was happy to have a friend. Baloo was just a sheer delight around Ian and also Justin when he arrived the following January.

We lived on five acres and I would let Baloo out to run around. One day I saw him on the back porch chewing on something. It was a tortoise. I got the poor thing out of Baloo's mouth, wiped off the slobber and set it free back on the acreage. He found several more and I had a secret suspicion it was the same unfortunate tortoise.

A couple of years flew by, and Bridgette was getting really old. She stopped eating, which was actually a first for this dog. At our previous house, before kids, David and I got the dogs an automatic dog feeder. Bridgette parked herself in front of the feeder. She would stand and eat or else lie down and eat. It was so convenient to shove her head inside the flapping door and eat. And eat. And eat. Bridgette gorged herself until she ballooned into a butterball Basset hound. The automatic dog feeder went away.

But now it was time. Sweet Bridgette was nearly 16 years old. It was late at night, so I took her to the animal emergency room. I loved and hugged and kissed on her. Sad, sad tears fell onto her. I told her how much I loved her. The vet had barely begun injecting the drugs that would send her over the Rainbow Bridge when sweet little Bridgette breathed her last breath. It was very peaceful and quiet and she knew I was there with her. She could see Daddy, Rusty, and Jake. I had Bridgette cremated and buried her next to Jake.

I actually put off getting another dog for a while since I had two young boys…and killer pit bulls across the street. I worried how Baloo would be without Bridgette. I know he missed her, but he adapted well to being an only dog. The boys adored him, and he was never, in his whole life, aggressive towards them. They climbed all over him, hugged him, sat by him, pulled out his hair as he blew his coat, and just loved that big old sweet boy. Baloo never growled or snapped at Ian or Justin.

Thoroughly assimilated into modern family life, the Pyrenean Mountain Dog is calm-natured and unaggressive, reliable in the home, and good with children. (9)

The only time he ever showed aggression was when something came up by the fence (like coyotes), or if somebody tried to get his French fries.

Baloo *loved* potatoes! He was thin for a Pyrenees and never weighed over 90 pounds, so I didn't mind feeding him potatoes. Baloo was never a greedy eater. His method of eating his dry kibble was to take a bite, run to the other side of the yard, eat it, run back to the bowl to get another mouthful, and start the process over. I should take eating lessons from Baloo!

He did become very wary of strange men. We had our yard sprayed for weeds, and the guy left the gate open. Baloo ran out and was promptly hit by a car on the busy street north of our house. I rushed him to the animal ER, and they recommended a surgeon who could fix his leg. His front left leg was broken, and the veterinarian had to put in a plate. I called the weed control company, and they said they were sorry, but they weren't paying for Baloo's surgery. Needless to say, I quit using their services. Mama paid for Baloo's surgery, for which I will always be grateful. For some reason, the veterinarian didn't put Baloo on antibiotics, so he developed an infection and the surgery had to be repeated, on the vet's dime.

In the spring of 2002, we moved due to financial reasons. Our new house had a huge yard for Baloo to run and play in. Across the street was a pasture with cows. At night we could hear coyotes. They came up by the fence one night and one night only. Baloo took care of business, even though he was on the other side of a stockade fence.

By summertime, Ian was ready to get a puppy. I had told him so much about Snoopy and showed him photos of Snoopy, that he decided he wanted a beagle puppy.

Since we had never neutered Baloo, I wanted to get another male dog. I know! I know! Spay and neuter your pets! I never planned on breeding Baloo, but I knew we needed all the testosterone we could get with our trashy neighbors. As calm as Baloo was, it was hard to tell that he wasn't neutered. And he never escaped and sired puppies.

I began scanning the newspaper ads for beagle puppies. I found an ad and as it turned out, the puppies were close to Okemah, in an even smaller town called Cromwell. And the breeder was the uncle of a good friend from high school!

The boys and I drove to Cromwell. Mr. Coker, the breeder, had already separated the girls from the boys as Ian wanted a male puppy. There were four boys, and, of course, we wanted all of them. I told Ian and Justin to sit on the floor and let the puppies come to them. Justin was only two and a half. Ian was almost seven.

One particular puppy kept running to Ian, and then over to Justin. He picked both of them! This was the one. Ian wanted to name him Rascal, so we scooped up Rascal and decided since we were so close to Valerie, in Okemah, we would go there to show him off.

Ian was so proud of Rascal. Rascal whined and cried some while he was sitting in the box in the car. Justin began crying and said Rascal missed his "brothays and sistays." (Justin couldn't say his "r's" and used an "ay" sound instead…until that and a slight lisp were corrected with speech therapy.)

That night Ian wanted Rascal to sleep in his room. Baloo slept outside. Everything was fine until Rascal began crying. And kept crying. Ian was not pleased. We tried everything. Pretty soon, David got up and walked back to Ian's room. He came back in a few minutes and put Rascal in bed with me. Rascal piped down and went to sleep. Mom, and Dad, for the win!

The next day David and I walked the fence line and plugged up beagle puppy-sized holes. Rascal was going to sleep outside with Baloo. Since it was summer, Rascal wasn't going to freeze to death.

The next morning when I woke up, I peered out the back door. Baloo was laying under the covered patio against the house. Rascal was curled up on top of him! Baloo couldn't have cared less about a new puppy, much less one piled on top of him snuggled down in his long white fur. It reminded me of the Looney Tunes cartoon with the bulldog and the kitten. I grabbed my new digital camera, which was advanced for the time, but not by today's standards at all. I slid the blinds open quietly and silently cursed that I hadn't washed my backdoor window (no housework gene, remember). I snapped a couple of photos anyway. One of them is framed and in my kitchen right now, 19 years later.

Beagles are happy dogs: happy to be hunting, happy to be home, happy to be with their people. This disposition explains only a part of the breed's tremendous popularity. Longevity, good looks, and intelligence are also notable pluses. OVER-VOCALIZATION and A TRACE OF STUBBORNNESS are cited by some owners as potential concerns. (10) (Emphasis is MINE!)

Baloo was never a big chewer. Rascal was a different story. When Rascal was about a year old, David and I got the boys a trampoline. We also got the safety net to put around it. We spent one whole Saturday putting the trampoline together and running the net around it, as well as covering the springs. While we were doing this, we had a radio plugged in outside. At one point, we heard a loud yelp and the music stopped playing. We looked up and Rascal was shaking his head and squeaking. He had just learned about the power of a wet tongue on a live electrical outlet. He was fine and, hopefully, he had learned a lesson. However, we looked up a little bit later and he was sniffing the plug again! David yelled at him and that did the trick.

The gas line to the grill wasn't as fortunate. One evening, David went out and the grill wouldn't start. He tried and tried to light it, then discovered why it wouldn't light: Rascal had chewed through the propane gas line! And it wouldn't be the last time, either! Did this beagle have an appointment with an early death? Did his mother squeeze too hard during his birth? What was so enticing about the gas line, other than blowing us all to smithereens?

After the third time Rascal snacked on the gas line, David wrapped chicken wire around the gas cannister and the base of the grill. It looked super attractive, like it was just off the showroom floor. It became a conversation piece whenever we had company and ate outside. Which brings up another obsession with Rascal…

We had an outdoor patio set, a table and six chairs. The straps on the chairs were flexible plastic strips. The chairs had cushions which covered the straps and tied to the chairs so they wouldn't slide around. Well, unless you have a beaver—I mean, a beagle—for a pet.

Yep. First, Rascal chewed all of the ties off the cushions. Then, he proceeded to chew nearly every strap on every chair. He left enough straps to hold the cushions, but we had to be very careful when we sat down so we wouldn't drop to the concrete floor. By the time we moved in 2015, we junked the chairs. We couldn't find anyone to replace the plastic straps. Chairs were being made with metal slats now. Probably because the owners of the companies owned beagles.

But Rascal didn't stop there. My friend Kathy, from church, told me I could come over to her house and dig up some redbud saplings. I love redbuds! Since they are Oklahoma's state tree, I needed to have one in my yard. Our housing addition had been built in a pasture and our particular area didn't have any trees in it. I spent a Sunday afternoon digging up a sizeable sapling and planted it in the backyard near the boys' sandpile (where Baloo buried food, such as slices of pizza).

The next day I went out to water the tree. All I found was a small, thin stump poking its sad little head out of the ground. As we were fresh out of beavers, I knew who the culprit was. I was furious! I did manage to plant a weeping willow and that thing prospered. Rascal and Baloo loved lying under it. But that was the extent of my landscaping for a while.

Rascal eventually outgrew his chewing phase, although the occasional flip flop was sacrificed, as well as a little stuffed kiwi bird Ian got when we went to New Zealand.

The boys and dogs thrived. On summer afternoons and evenings, we would sit outside and the boys would play in their sand box. Baloo blew his coat in the summer, and the boys and I loved to sit next to him and pull out his fine tufts of hair that had turned loose. Our yard looked like it had snowed. Birds would fly over, swoop down, and grab his hair for their nests.

When 2010 rolled around, Baloo began developing tumors on his rear end, particularly around his anus. I took him to the vet and they removed them. That seemed to help. They also x-rayed him to make sure there weren't any more tumors inside him. Luckily there weren't.

During this time, I happened to stop at Petco. They were having a dog adoption, and I saw a Catahoula dog. He was a really sweet and cool dog. I thought it would be a good idea to get another dog so when Baloo left this earth, Rascal would have another friend. I told Ian and Justin about him and, of course they were on board. We just didn't tell David.

We went to the Edmond Animal Shelter to check him out. He had already been adopted. Thankfully. We did see two puppies that looked like Redbone Coonhounds (it's starting…) and they were named Dan and Ann. Remember *Where the Red Fern Grows*? Well, we picked out Dan.

These two puppies had been found by the side of the road, obviously dumped by some low life. They had longer hair, so I know they weren't full blood Redbones but they were sure cute. Dan was adopted by the Jaynes, and his name became Scout.

David was not thrilled but soon appreciated the hard, little life Scout had already lived. What we didn't realize was that Scout had not been social-ized. We had him from September through December. And in December, Scout attacked Rascal and tore open Rascal's shoulder. We took Rascal to the animal emergency room because, of course, it was after hours at our vet. Scout went to our vet the next day to be boarded until we could find another home for him. I couldn't take the chance on Scout attacking Ian or Justin, but I couldn't bring myself to take him back to the dog pound. I was having surgery the next day, so boarding him at our vet was the only option.

And just to let you know how things went, during my surgery, a benign lumpectomy, I was diagnosed with atrial fibrillation. So, after surgery, I went to the Oklahoma Heart Hospital for an I.V. of Corevert, which would convert me back to a regular sinus rhythm, like it did for David a few months earlier when he had developed heart flutter.

Nothing is ever easy, whether it's our attempt to save a dog from the pound, or figuring out I'm a medical outlier. The simple I.V. drip to convert me back to a regular heart rhythm put me into full cardiac arrest. For two minutes. Two shocks with the paddles. Needless to say, Scout stayed at the vet a few more days.

Luckily, a friend from church knew a family in western Oklahoma who lived on a farm and were looking for a dog. Scout got to go live on a farm. They loved him but said he wasn't so sure about their cats. Justin and I cried and cried when Scout left, and I apologized to him. But I didn't want Rascal attacked again. Or my boys. We still saved Scout, but now he was on a farm!

Meanwhile, something wasn't right with Baloo. He was now 11-1/2 years old, and began having small bouts of paralysis. He would be out in the yard and then he would fall to the ground and couldn't get up for a while. His tumors had grown back. I had a sneaking suspicion he had tumors in his spine. Maybe his brain.

On the night of February 4, 2011, it was particularly cold. I brought the dogs in the house and put them in our laundry room. When I went to check on Baloo, the towels he was lying on had blood on them. There were blood spatters on the wall, too. My old guy looked at me with a sad, sad look.

Like he was saying, "I'm so sorry, Mom. I didn't mean to. I love you, Mom. But. It's. Time."

No. It can't be time. This sweet old dog who loves my boys so much can't leave. This dog—who helped me up when my back went out (bending over to pick up a dog food bowl) by letting me rest against him and hold on to his back as I stood up—can't leave. He just can't. I'm not ready. He's too sweet. He needs more time with me. And my family. And Rascal.

But I knew what I had to do. David carried Baloo to our Expedition. The boys and I climbed in. We took Rascal, too. He needed to say good-bye to his brother. With the exception of the first six weeks of his life, he'd never been away from Baloo.

Since it was late at night, as always, we went to the animal emergency room. Ian didn't want to be there when Baloo died, so he and David waited in the lobby with Rascal. Justin, who was barely 11, went into the room with Baloo and me. Baloo had known Justin while Justin was still in utero. He'd always been with Justin. And now he was leaving.

I got down in the floor with my big old white fluffy dog while the veterinarian administered the lethal drugs that would send my sweet pet to heaven. Justin and I cried and told Baloo how much we loved him. Baloo drifted off with his big old sweet head on his front legs. His front paws were on my legs.

All of my dogs have been special, but Baloo won the prize. I think more of my heart went with him than with the other dogs to whom I'd said good-bye. I'd gotten him to protect my boys. And he had. He did his job. He was a good boy.

Ian and David brought Rascal in to see Baloo. Rascal sniffed him and seemed to know that Baloo was gone. I stayed a little while longer. We had to leave even though I didn't want to leave my Baloo. My last glimpse of that great dog was seeing him lying on the floor, his head on his paws, and his big, brown eyes closed like he was sleeping. He looked like a big, brave, white lion. I whispered "I love you" to him and told him I'd see him again.

I truly believe our pets go to heaven. Remember that God saved animals during the flood. He tells us that we can't imagine what heaven is like. I can't imagine heaven without animals.

...but just as it is written, "Things which eye has not seen and ear has not heard, and which have not entered the heart of man, all that God has prepared for those who love Him."

I Corinthians 2:9

Who will meet us first in Heaven? Jesus? Our family? Or will our pets race Jesus to the gates made of pearl to see us?

The drive home was quiet. Rascal stuck close to the boys. And every night Rascal rotated sleeping with the boys. One night he would be in Ian's bed at his feet, and the next night he would be sleeping with Justin in his bed. We'd never allowed the dogs to sleep in the bed with us (although I let Rusty sleep with me before I married David). But I made an executive decision, and Rascal was now free to hop on the boys' beds and sleep with them. I felt like Rascal needed my boys as much as they needed him. After all, the only canine brother he had ever known was gone.

The next few days were snowy and cold. School was cancelled because of the snow and it was almost a blessing. We hung out at the house, and Rascal never left our side. I know he enjoyed the attention but we were all sad. In a funk. When the boys finally got to go back to school, I let Rascal out in the yard for some fresh air.

And just like I heard Bridgette mourn and howl for Rusty, Rascal began to howl like I had never heard him howl before. Normally he and Baloo would howl at sirens. This was different. It was mournful. He wasn't "singing." Rascal was crying. And for a couple of nights, Rascal would go outside and bark a different bark. He was searching for Baloo and letting him know where he was. Rascal was calling to Baloo and waiting for an answer that wouldn't come.

In the days following, I would pick up tufts of Baloo's fur that were in the yard, and wondered how many bird nests were lined with his fur. A working dog's work is never done. He's keeping baby birds warm. I put his big pink food bowl in the cushion holder. I've never let another dog eat out of it. Is that silly? I don't know. Dog people understand. Maybe it's just a bit of "sacredness" to me and respect for Baloo.

I had Baloo cremated but I have never buried him. At some point we knew we would move, and I wanted him to go with us. I'd thought about placing some of his remains in one of the spots in the yard where he always liked to lie down and sleep. But I didn't. He's still with me and perhaps someday I'll lay him to rest and plant a tree over him. But for now, he goes with me. To date, he's gone with me through two moves. Maybe when I'm gone, Baloo can be sprinkled in with me.

Good boy, Baloo. Good boy.

Chapter 4

More Beagles

A sturdy, compact dog with a merry disposition, the Beagle looks rather like an English Foxhound in miniature...This versatile hound has also been used by law enforcement agencies to sniff out drugs, explosives, and other illegal items. (11)

I know this book is about rescuing coonhounds. I *promise* I'll get to coonhounds in the next chapter!

Since Justin had never picked out his very own dog before, it was his turn. We talked about dogs and spent an afternoon at Barnes and Noble looking at books detailing dog breeds, some of which I'd never seen before. After much discussion, and prayer, Justin decided he wanted a...hold on... *beagle.* I was hardly surprised.

We waited until it was spring break so Justin could spend time with his new puppy. Once again, I began scouring the ads for beagle puppies. Rascal's breeder had passed away, so there was no chance of us getting another one of his puppies. I found two ads for beagle puppies. Naturally they weren't in Edmond. One was in Shawnee, and I can't remember where the other one was. It doesn't matter because we went to Shawnee first "just to look," and do you really think we wouldn't bring home a beagle puppy from the first litter of puppies we saw?

Actually, when Ian was looking for his puppy, David and I took the boys to a place that had beagle puppies. Well, they may have been *part* beagle. The place was nasty and the dogs didn't look well. The last thing I wanted was to get a puppy who was going to require a lot of veterinary care and possibly die. And none of those puppies really warmed up to Ian; one didn't "pick him out." If one had, it might have been a completely different story.

The boys and I set out for Shawnee. I called the owner to tell him we were on our way. He said he'd be there as soon as he could but if we got there first, the puppies were in a pen in the backyard and we were welcome to get in there and play with them. Awesome marketing tip.

We arrived at his house, which was on a neat, clean, green acreage. The owner wasn't there. That was probably intentional. Marketing, remember? We walked back to the dog pen. Well, Justin ran towards it. We saw three little white tails bobbing toward the gate. Justin and Ian and I stepped inside the pen. One little puppy immediately ran to the other side of the pen. He would not come up to us. But there were two others who wouldn't leave the boys alone. Justin picked up a little male and the puppy wagged his tail furiously and licked Justin all over the face.

Ian held a little girl and immediately wanted to get her and name her Lucille. She was affectionate, too. But I only had enough money for one puppy. And it was Justin's choice.

On the way to Shawnee, we had been thinking of names for the new puppy. Ian was reading Greek mythology and began reading names of gods and warriors.

"Blah blah blah, Ajax, blah blah blah…"

Ajax!

Justin decided on the male. Ajax. By that time the beagle breeder arrived (well-played, Dude). He had bred beagles for decades. We went inside his clean little office, and he gave Ajax a shot of wormer and his registration papers (which I never sent in). He asked Justin what he was going to name the puppy, and Justin told him, "Ajax" and then expounded on how he came up with that name.

It was time for us to leave. I was really wishing I'd brought more money to buy Lucille. (What was I thinking?) But David would have killed me. And Rascal probably wasn't going to be in the mood for *two* puppies.

The boys took turns holding Ajax on the way home. We almost made it home without having to stop. But then Ajax decided he needed to poop. Justin was yelling at me to stop and even turned Ajax upside down, as if the poop would go back in! I found a place to pull over and Justin's first job as an official pet owner was to get out with Ajax while the puppy pooped. Justin also learned he wasn't going to die with a little puppy poop on his jeans.

We made it home and Rascal's nose was immediately out of joint. Not only had he lost his best friend a few weeks previously, but now there was an infiltrator in the house.

At bedtime, Rascal was more than happy to sleep with Ian. We put a box with blankets next to Justin's bed for Ajax to sleep in. I went to bed. I was almost asleep when Justin came into my room telling me he couldn't sleep because Ajax was yelping. I told him to hang his arm in the box. Didn't work. Guess who slept in the recliner with a beagle puppy on her chest? The only female in the house. Mom! Justin had a great night's sleep. As did Ajax. Mine was okay.

Things settled down and we decided to convert the sand box into a garden. We had some nice dirt hauled in. Manure was mixed in it. Great soil for a garden!

David and I spent a whole afternoon shoveling the dirt into wheelbarrows and wheeling it into the backyard. Then we put up a wire fence around it, complete with a gate. While we were hauling the dirt, the boys and dogs played in it. Ajax and Rascal dug and dug and dug. Ajax sniffed the dirt constantly and had a brown nose.

As David and I worked and worked, the boys and dogs played elsewhere in the yard. Pretty soon I looked up and couldn't find Ajax. Where was he?

We looked and looked and finally found him lying against the stockade fence. He wasn't moving. I checked his gums and they were whitish.

It was the weekend, so we had to go to the animal ER. Again. Story of our lives. The diagnosis was that Ajax had spent so much time in the manure-enriched dirt, and dug in it and sniffed it and probably ate some of it, that he had ingested some protozoa, which made him extremely sick. He recovered but was not allowed in the garden again. We had to make sure the gate was closed at all times.

Ajax didn't chew up things the way Rascal did. He did, however, get extremely carsick. I had to put towels down on every square inch of our Expedition, and Ajax always managed to find the one little patch of carpet not covered by a towel to puke on. But he didn't stop with puking. He pooped in the car, too!

Trips to the vet became a challenge for me to see if I could beat the time from the last trip without getting pulled over or cleaning out puke and poop. Most of the time I made it. Almost. Just as I pulled into the vet's parking lot,

I'd hear Ajax heaving in a sliver of a corner not covered by a towel. We had to make sure he was not given any kind of treat before we took him somewhere. But that did not mean he didn't find food on his own.

After one trip to the vet, Ajax threw up on the way home. Actually, as we pulled into the driveway. Yours truly was the official puke and poop and pee cleaner-upper but this time there was a twist. What was, surprisingly, on the towel, was a former critter, with hind legs and a little fur left. Seems like Mr. Ajax had caught, and eaten, and enjoyed a field rat before his little jaunt to the vet.

I cleaned the car out as best as I could, and then David and I took it to get it detailed. We told the kid who worked there we needed the carpets cleaned because the dog had thrown up on the carpet.

"We can't clean your car," he told us. Unbeknownst to us, they aren't allowed, or just don't want to mess with, bodily fluids. I told him this was dog puke; I hadn't killed anyone! It didn't matter.

I cleaned the car out myself and then later we went to another place and had it detailed, omitting the detail of rat-infused beagle vomit.

Ajax could probably warrant his very own book. He is highly entertaining. And he is the beagle who allowed me to see how flat out *weird* these dogs can be. And manipulative. And *sssstttttttuuuubbbbboooorrrrnnnn*. Oh, I forgot. Just a "trace of stubbornness" like the dog book says. Rascal had his stubborn moments, but Ajax takes the cake. Takes the cake and *eats* the cake. Maybe even pukes up the cake.

The following January, we had the coldest night on record. Minus 10 degrees and falling.

I had let the dogs out to go to the bathroom. When I called them back in (I usually didn't even have to do that, as Rascal would be barking at the door), no one came running. I went out on the patio and yelled for them.

Nothing. I ran around to the north side of the house and saw that the gate was open! They were gone!

I ran in yelling that the dogs were gone and everyone put on their coats. David took Justin in one car while Ian and I hopped in the Expedition. Off we went with our windows down in sub-zero weather, hollering for Rascal and Ajax. Add to it that in such cold weather, the pressure gauge on the tires of the Expedition registered an alarm, so it went off, literally, every minute. To the east of our housing addition was a pasture with cows and sheep. To the west, across the neighborhood, was another pasture with cows. There was a vacant lot so people, animals, and *beagles* could easily pass through.

We looked. We yelled. We prayed. At times I'd stop and try to listen. I could hear a dog bark, and it sounded like Rascal. We drove up and down the busy roads next to our addition, hoping we wouldn't find our dogs dead or dying on the side of the road. I kept thinking I heard Rascal. Several times. It was always after we yelled for them. And just before the tire alarm sounded.

After what seemed an eternity, David called, and he and Justin had the dogs! They were on the west side of the addition and were calling for them when Rascal barked and ran out to meet them. He hopped right in the car; Ajax wasn't as willing as he was enjoying the adventure.

I was so glad to see our dogs, even though they smelled like cow poop! Evidently on their midnight excursion, they headed straight for the cow pasture and to their delight, there was poop to roll in!

To this day I don't know if the wind blew open the gate or if Ajax finagled around and got it open. We were thrilled and grateful to have them home. I really would have liked to have had a beagle camera on them!

There weren't any more running away adventures until we moved to our current house. (And it's a really good story you can enjoy later in Chapter 10.) We had decided to fix up our house and maybe try to sell it. David rented a "pod" to store things in while we put down hardwood floors and repainted the whole house. The very next day, a man rang our doorbell, and we assumed it was the floor guy or the painter. Nope. He saw the pod and asked if we were moving because he was looking for a house in our neighborhood and could he come in and look around? We told him our plans and he said he could do the painting and hardwood floors himself. Well good for you. He looked around, and two hours later, he called to see if he could bring his wife to look at the house! She came out, and they made us an offer, asking when we could move out! (They were living with their three small boys at her parents' house. David said that man must have decided he was buying a house *today*!) I wanted to ask if I could grab a pair of clean underwear before they took over because they were ready to kick us out right then and there.

I told him we needed *at least* six weeks. The wife pulled up her calendar and said that would be May 15. Deal. What? Wait! Needless to say, we got in gear and got rid of lots of crap (which could be another book). Our friends from church owned houses, so we rented one from them. They also had an acreage, and I moved Harry, my horse, to their place. (During all of this commotion, Susan, my friend and horse trainer, died unexpectedly.)

In May of 2015, we moved to our cozy little rent house, with Ajax and Rascal in tow. And since things weren't complicated enough, we had rescued a senior beagle for David's parents for Christmas. They were in assisted living and really wanted a dog, so we took them to a beagle rescue and they picked out—well, she picked them out—a very small lemon and white beagle named Marilyn. Who became Daisy. Then Honey. Literally, every time we went to visit, they had changed this poor dog's name. Finally, they settled on a name and she officially became Lucy.

In March of 2016, David's dad, who had dementia, got jealous because David's mom was paying more attention to Lucy than him. Again, here's another book, as my mother has dementia, and it's a new day every two minutes. I refused to take Lucy back to the rescue, so our beagle pack grew to three.

Now, I've told you how scared Rusty was of thunder. But if you put her in the house or garage, she was fine. Settled right down. Lucy needed a ThunderShirt. And lavender oil. And drugs. *HARD* drugs. Prescription drugs. Drugs with a high street value. And double the dosage.

She absolutely panicked. We had to hold her until we fell asleep or her drugs finally kicked in. But she would get so worked up, it took a while. (The thought of us actually taking her drugs crossed our minds. We could at least rest and wouldn't know if Lucy was freaking out or not.) When there was even a chance of thunder, out came the pills. I know that sounds awful, but Lucy was beyond terrified.

In fact, Lucy was terrified of just about everything. I don't know what kind of abusive past this poor little dog had had, but it must have been ugly. The rescue people thought she might have been caught out in the F5 tornado that hit the Moore/Norman area in 2013. That would certainly explain her fear of storms. I don't blame her. Loud noises made her jump. Walking past her made her jump. Doors scared her, and it took what seemed like an eternity before I could get her to walk on her own through the back door. Maybe she'd been kicked. Maybe she'd been caged. I don't know, but I do know that we had to put a leash on her to drag—uh, lead—her through the back door. She was as sweet as she could be, but literally scared of her own shadow. I watched her jump and whine one day when a *leaf* rustled by her! However, Lucy didn't give a flip about Ajax or Rascal.

Rascal had been diagnosed with Cushing's Disease; a kidney disease common in beagles. He started getting incontinent and dribbled urine. The veterinarian prescribed Proin; we called them his "pee pills."

We always find out what's common in beagles *after* our beagles contract it. Another case in point: beagles are susceptible to ACL tears. Ajax helped us discover this. After his surgery, one of our veterinarians, Dr. Erik Eldridge, said that within a year, beagles will usually tear the other ACL. Want to hazard a guess what happened to Ajax about a year later?

Meanwhile, Lucy had a couple of ER visits for not eating. So, after spending a gazillion dollars to determine she had not one, but *five* abscessed teeth, we got to spend a gazillion more dollars to extract the teeth. Add to that kidney problems for her, as well. Lucy couldn't have protein, so we got to buy her $3.00/can special KD dog food. Of course, Ajax and Rascal wanted *that* dog food instead of theirs. Too bad, so sad. Eat your kibble.

Since Lucy was nearly toothless, we didn't have much choice as to what she could eat. And then when I'd start to gripe a little, I imagined what kind of life she had had. And what kind of care she would have gotten had she not been rescued, and had we not adopted her. None. She would have been dumped. Or starved to death.

Anyway, we continued along in our little rent house, and in the summer of 2016, we rented a beach house in Gulf Shores, Alabama. Justin's friend, Caleb, dog sat for us.

We got home on July 2, Rascal's 14th birthday. The next day Rascal was paralyzed. He couldn't get up. He tried. Then he stopped trying. Still, being a beagle, he didn't want anyone picking him up. Beagle people know this. Ian wrapped his beloved old Rascal in a towel, and the four Jaynes took him to the animal ER. Because it was at night, after hours, a holiday, and our vet was closed. Because, of course.

The prognosis was dire. The veterinarian felt around and squeezed on Rascal. Nothing. Rascal couldn't feel it. There was only one decision we could make. That perfectly horrible decision that every pet owner hates to make. It was time for Rascal to cross the Rainbow Bridge into heaven and go be with Baloo.

Gulp. I thank God that we made it home from vacation and that Caleb didn't have to deal with this. I think Rascal was waiting for us to come home. And now we were home and we were telling our beloved beagle, Ian's very first pet, good-bye.

It's always hard for me to have a pet put to sleep. But what was really hard was watching Ian and Justin, through their tears, tell Rascal how much they loved him. Rascal had picked these boys out. They were his. He was theirs.

As we petted Rascal, the tears flowed. I scooped up some of his hair and put it in my pocket.

Ian was bent over Rascal so Rascal could see him. Huge tears softly fell out of Ian's eyes and slid ever so slowly down his cheeks. And there was nothing I could do as a mother to help my son feel better. Nothing. At. All.

We were with Rascal while the dreaded medicine did its job. He stopped breathing and laid on the examination table like he was asleep.

What a good boy Rascal was. We had been telling him that. And how very much we loved him. He knew and he took that love with him. I truly believe animals go to heaven. Now Daddy had another dog with him, and Rascal was with his beloved Baloo.

We had Rascal cremated. Ever since we moved out of the house we built, I've had my pets cremated and they move with me.

The next day was the Fourth of July. It was a melancholy one for us. A very quiet one. We sat on the porch of our rent house and watched fireworks from the nearby Oklahoma Christian University, where Ian attended college. But we weren't very excited.

A few days later I picked up Rascal's remains. The company that cremated him made a clay impression of Rascal's footprint. I had to giggle a little bit because Rascal *hated* for anyone to touch his feet. No trimming his nails. No rubbing his feet. No checking for ticks between his toe pads. But now I have an impression of one of his feet. The feet that happily ran from Ian to Justin the day we got him. The feet that followed the boys everywhere. The feet that ran around the trampoline with the boys. The feet that went on a midnight excursion in sub-zero temperature with Mr. Ajax. The feet that carried him to your side in a flash when standing near the treat jar. The feet that trotted over to you and let him slide up for a belly rub like a beached seal when you were sitting on the floor. The feet we would no longer hear clicking on the wood or tile floor.

We were looking for a house and soon found one with which we all fell in love. It was on 1-1/4 acre and had everything we wanted in a house, including a pool. Plus, deer were everywhere, as it is near Arcadia Lake and is surrounded by undeveloped land. I'm praying the land north of us stays undeveloped.

On September 17, 2016, we moved into this house. Ajax and Lucy explored, and there were a zillion more things that frightened little Lucy. There is an outdoor fireplace made out of brown stone and Texas limestone. Lucy enjoyed sitting by the fireplace, basking in the sun. Lucy blended in perfectly when she sat in front of the fireplace and was perfectly camouflaged, to the point of almost being invisible.

The really big thing for Lucy was when she discovered, on her own, that our master bathroom and closet were in the middle of the house. No windows. It is very dark when the lights are off. That became her safe room for thunderstorms! No more panting or freaking out or drugs or ThunderShirts or lavender oil. At the first rumble of thunder, Lucy checked herself into our bathroom and curled up on one of the rugs. We shut the doors, and that was that!

We settled in to our new house and had our first round of fall and winter holidays. Deer were plentiful and I fed them corn every day. Harry, my horse was an eight-minute drive away. Things were "normal." How was I to know that very soon, God would send a coonhound my way?

Chapter 5

God Sent a Coonhound

Do not withhold good from those to whom it is due,
when it is in your power to do it.

Proverbs 3:27

It was June 21, 2017. Just an average summer day. I had gone to see Valerie in Okemah. I don't remember why I had gone, but for whatever reason, it was now time for me to head back to Edmond.

I was at Valerie's house. Her daughter, Andrea, and her grandsons, Camden and Cale, were also there. They live three blocks away. As we walked to my car, we saw a dog trotting up the street.

Camden said it looked like his friend's dog. We began calling to the dog and he came right over to us. Camden informed us that this was not his friend's dog.

This dog was a Treeing Walker Coonhound. And he was skin and bones. His ribs were sticking out so much I could put my fingers between them. His hip bones were sticking out. His vertebrae were sticking out. There was a big gash on his right side behind his front leg and a large raw spot on his neck. He didn't have a collar. I know he had been tied up with a rope or chain to make that raw spot. He had either been dumped or managed to escape. But he was sweet and loving to us. He jumped right up on me.

Valerie ran in the house and got some food and water for this poor dog. He drank the water first, then gobbled up the food. My mind was already racing.

The coonhound walked around a little and looked at Valerie's dogs through their chain link fence. Then he started to trot up the street. He made it across the street to the Baptist Church and I couldn't stand it. Something inside me said not to let this dog get away. I called to him, and he came back to me, promptly jumping up on me and giving me my first coonhound hug. (Andrea took a photo and that is the cover of this book.)

I started to cry.

Andrea called the veterinarian to see if I could bring him out to get the gash sewn up. No one answered. No one was supposed to answer. Because I was supposed to take this coonhound home with me. I know now that God sent this dog to me.

Still crying, I texted David and told him I was bringing home a starving dog who is skin and bones. No response. In my heart I knew this would not go over well. But in my heart, I also knew I couldn't leave this dog, this sweet, sweet hound, to starve in the streets. Oh well. He was coming with me anyway.

Valerie got an old pillow for the dog to lie on in the floorboard so that blood wouldn't get everywhere. Since I'm a yoga teacher, I have mats and yoga straps with me. I got a yoga strap out of the car and made a leash.

The dog appeared never to have walked on a leash, so we had to drag him to the car. Maybe he had never ridden in a car, or had just been dumped and wasn't eager to get back in a car. Whatever had or had not happened, this coonhound didn't want to get in the car. We coaxed and pulled and pushed until he got in. We put him on the nice soft pillow in the floorboard. By the time I got around to my side, Mr. Coonhound had hopped up and was sitting shotgun in the passenger seat.

I reasoned with myself that I could get the bloodstains out of the leather seat. What's more important is that this guy is comfortable. I waved good-bye to everyone and drove off. As I drove away, the coonhound decided he would be better suited in my lap. I gently pushed him back to his seat. He tried one more time and when that didn't work, he curled up in a ball in the seat and went to sleep in a "coonie curl." You'll find out more about them later.

My mind raced. Who had been so cruel to this dog? Who starves an animal? What is David going to say? Was this dog tied up with a rope or chained? Will I get alimony in the divorce? How long has this poor dog been fending for himself on the street? What has he been able to find to eat? Will Justin want to live with me or David? What am I going to name this dog?

If you name an animal, it becomes yours. You know that, don't you? This is a hound dog. He needs a good name. A strong name. My mind traveled back to all of the hounds I had been around, the ones you just read about. The beagles, the foxhounds, the Basset hound. I remember some of the names of the beagles Grandpa Casey had: Sue, Screamer (I know this to be very fitting for a beagle now that we have Ajax), Mutt, and Jeff. Those were the four I was the most familiar with. Grandpa Casey sure loved his beagles.

Hmmm. Grandpa Casey. Franklin Martin Casey. F.M. Casey. Was this hound dog a Frank? A Martin? A Mart? A Marty?

No. Not really. Even though these were all names that people called Grandpa Casey.

Casey?

I said it out loud.

"Casey."

YES!

So that was that. I had a coonhound named Casey. I began to talk to him, calling him Casey. And I also began to thank God for sending Casey to me, for sending me to Casey, for Casey not to ever have to be hungry again, or to not ever have a soft place to sleep, or not to ever be on the street again. Oh, and while you're at it, God, please don't let David kick me out of the house.

Casey sniffed my travel mug of water. I popped off the lid and he helped himself, lapping up some water. My, what a big tongue you have, I thought, as water drops rained everywhere. I can use them to wipe up the blood that I just knew was sinking into my leather car seat.

I petted Casey and told him what a good boy he was. Dogs like to hear that. They really do. I wondered if anyone had ever told Casey that he was a good boy. I doubted it, and my heart cracked a little.

With the exception of lapping up more water, Casey spent the car ride curled up and resting. Perhaps this was the first time in a long time, if ever, that he felt safe. Luckily, he wasn't puking his guts up, or pooping, like his soon-to-be-brother does in the car. Casey had one more drink, as the travel mug was officially his now, until I could pop it in the dishwasher.

When we got home, it was close to dusk. I led Casey through the house and into the back yard. David was in the pool. He watched me lead Casey across the patio, open the gate, and lead him over the purple bridge to the dog pen.

The people who used to live here built a bridge, a *purple* bridge, to cross the rocky creek bed that separates the back yard from the side yard. They had also built a brick dog house that is about 10 feet by 14 feet with a doggy door, to access the large, fenced pen. There is a full-sized door to enter the dog house, which is complete with a ceiling fan and an air conditioner. Since it was a warm summer night with no chance of rain, Casey could spend the night in the dog pen and the next day I would introduce him to Ajax and Lucy.

Casey ran around the pen and explored. I sat down and he ran up to me for some love. When he went back to running around, I slipped out to get some dog food and a bucket of water.

My departure didn't go unnoticed. Casey barked and howled the entire time I was gone. He stopped when I got back to the pen. He ate most of the food I brought him. I brought the pillow Valerie gave me for him to sleep on, so I sat there on the pillow with him for a while. Casey tried to get in my lap.

Justin and Ian got home from work. I had texted them about Casey. They came directly out to the dog pen to see their new dog—oh yeah, he's staying. Casey acted like they were his long-lost brothers. They got coonhound hugs, too.

Treeing Walker Coonhound: It is a dog that appreciates a friendly home environment and loves people. (12)

I stayed with Casey, hoping he would settle down. He stayed by me and I talked to him. It was starting to get dark. Every time I tried to leave, Casey went nuts. And then the sprinklers came on.

I made an executive decision to bring Casey in the house. He needed to meet Ajax and Lucy. Casey had no problem with Ajax. But when he saw Lucy, his eyes brightened and his ears perked up. Because Casey was intact. Unneutered. With testosterone. All. Male. He strutted over and pawed at Lucy as if to say, "Hey, Baby! Where have you been all my life?"

Little Lucy, sweet little Lucy, afraid of her own shadow, lunged at Casey and made one of the most vicious growls I'd ever heard from a little dog. She bared her teeth. Her hackles were up. Her soft brown eyes projected nothing but sheer rage. My little timid lemon and white rescue beagle was now a full-fledged saber-toothed tiger. She was having none of it. She had been spayed, and therefore, was definitely not in the mood. She was not impressed by, literally, the new stud in town.

Casey backed off. He was smart, although he did try a couple more times, getting the same reaction from Lucy. Ajax, on the other hand, was fascinated with Casey's testicles. Since Ajax was neutered when he was six months old (we had Rascal neutered at the same time), testicles were a foreign concept to him. It had been about six years since Ajax had been around any dog testicles.

He followed Casey everywhere. Casey didn't seem to mind, not even the constant sniffing. They looked like tri-colored fraternal twins. Casey looked just like a tall beagle. In fact, everyone who sees him thinks he is a large beagle.

I have never had a coonhound before. Several years ago, I was in Okemah and I was out at my brother-in-law's farm. A starving, skinny Treeing Walker Coonhound with cuts and scrapes on his bony back (sound familiar?) came up to us. He was whining and wagging his tail. Someone zipped into town and got some dog food and brought it back out. He gobbled it up, wagging his tail, squeaking the entire time. Valerie and Brett kept him and named him Copper. They had him for a while until one of their friends wanted him. Copper was a sweetheart, as I believe all coonhounds are. Anyway, I digress.

I was fascinated watching Casey as he trotted around the yard. His trot was like he was on springs. And he was constantly looking up. Raccoons. He was looking for raccoons.

I assumed, correctly, that he wasn't housebroken. He had probably never been in a house. He had already marked a door casing as "his territory" and won a free trip into the yard. It was a nice evening, and we have a dog house with three old sheepskin rugs in it, and lounge chairs with nice soft cushions on the patio. He could spend the night outside and get used to his new home. Ajax and Lucy would stay inside.

No worries.

Until bedtime.

When I was almost asleep.

The barking began.

The deep barking.

Mixed with some bays.

And howls.

While I appreciate a good hound dog song, I didn't think the neighbors on either side of us would appreciate a coonhound serenade. Especially late at night.

Off our master bedroom, we have a sun room that has a door to the patio. I got up and sat outside with Casey. I put a collar on him, one I had gotten for Rascal that was too big. I snapped a leash on it and sat on the patio with Casey at my side. He was perfectly happy to have me pet him. He enjoyed putting his front legs in my lap and standing on his hind legs, since that was the next best thing to actually being in my lap.

When Casey would settle down, I would unsnap the leash. Off he'd run, barking. Off I'd go after him, snapping the leash back on him and leading him back to the patio. This happened several times.

I knew the neighbors would only listen to a deep and constant bark for so long, whether it was night or day. My heart grew heavy. Would I have to find a new home for Casey? After only one day, Casey was part of the family. I couldn't let him go.

I sent messages to my friends who hunt and told them about Casey. They bird hunt so they use Labradors or pointers. They also hunt deer, but you can't hunt deer with dogs. No one hunted raccoons. No one needed a

Treeing Walker Coonhound. I knew that I was keeping him. We'd figure something out about the barking.

Enter God. Again.

David had already ordered a shock collar. Before you get all bent out of shape, we only set it to vibrate, *NEVER* to shock. As I said, Casey is a smart dog. He did not like the vibration, so it didn't take long for him to stop barking. Patience and persistence paid off. Whenever the collar vibrated, Casey came over to us so that we would pet him.

Since coonhounds do their raccoon-chasing business at night, and I had to get some sleep so I could go to work the next day, I brought Casey inside. I snapped the leash on him and scooted a dog bed over by the couch. I encouraged Casey to lie down in the dog bed while I held the leash. We had just gotten a new couch. No dogs were allowed on the couch. Remember this. File this information away.

Casey laid in the dog bed, and I got a lump in my throat. This was probably the first soft bed he had had in a long time. If ever. I'm sure the monster who previously owned him kept him tied up, and a tree or old barrel was his only shelter. Soft beds are hard to come by when you're a street dog. I doubt if Casey had ever been in a house before, much less slept inside one.

When you lie down, you will not be afraid;
when you lie down, your sleep will be sweet.

Proverbs 3:24

He got up several times during the night. I'd take him outside, and then we would come back in, and I'd have him lie on his bed. Finally, we were both sound asleep. Casey was a smart dog, so I only had to spend three nights on the couch.

The next morning, I called our vet and scheduled Casey for his vaccinations, worming, to have the gash in his side checked, and to check him for heart worms. They told me to bring him in that afternoon.

DING! DING! DING! We have a winner! Casey is positive for heart worms! What a shock. Since I had decided that Casey was all mine, I opted for the longer—but much less expensive—monthly heart worm treatment.

I also scheduled—insert ominous bell tolls—a date for neutering the following Monday. The veterinarian told me to put Polysporin on Casey's gash until I brought him in to be neutered. He would stitch the gash up at the same time. He added that I was to keep him from licking off the Polysporin. Sounds good in theory.

We only had a couple of days until his "life-altering" surgery. I put the Polysporin on Casey's gash. Approximately five minutes later, Casey was licking his wound, removing any trace of Polysporin. It was impossible to keep Casey from licking the medicine off his gash, especially since I was at work during much of the day. I figured that since he had been on his own long enough, and who knows when he got the gash, and what he had been exposed to, he wouldn't die from an infection.

Casey didn't die from any infection. And the neutering and wound-stitching went well. The veterinarian stitched the gash up right on a line between black hair and white hair. It didn't even leave a scar. No one could even tell there had been a gaping hole there.

We had the barking under control, but Casey was still trying to get in our laps. And he would jump up on us. Casey had to learn not to jump up on people. Coonhounds tree raccoons, and to an extent, *climb* trees in pursuit of said raccoons. They will rear up on their hind legs, put their front paws on the tree, and bay to let their owner know there is a raccoon in the tree. To Casey, *we* were the trees!

And while I didn't mind Casey using me as a "tree" and giving me hugs, this was a habit that had to be broken. David and I both had elderly parents. The last thing they needed was a broken hip from a coonhound hugging them. Knees to the chest and a loud "OFF!" worked on Casey after a few days.

This stray Treeing Walker Coonhound had made his way into our hearts. I knew I would *never ever* think of finding another home for Casey. His place in our family was solidified. Casey was a Jayne.

Little Lucy's life got easier, too. No more coonhound-induced foreplay or romancing. No more Caseynova to contend with! (See what I did there?)

The next day my world got rocked.

Ian showed me a Facebook post from a woman in Okemah. It was a "Have you seen this dog?" post. A "Have you seen this dog?" with Casey's photo post. We were horrified.

My heart sank.

Ian asked me what we were going to do. I mean, if Casey belonged to this girl, and she was looking for him, I needed to give him back, right?

Well, no, I didn't. Did she let him get this skinny? Did she tie him up and cause the raw, bald spot on his neck? She doesn't deserve this dog back. Too bad if she's looking for her starving coonhound. And if she's going to breed him, good luck with that, as the family jewels were gone. I had already made up my mind that I wasn't giving Casey back.

No. Way.

Chapter 6

ARLO

Open your mouth for the mute, for the rights of the unfortunate. Open your mouth, judge righteously, and defend the rights of the afflicted and needy.

Proverbs 31: 8-9

The Animal Rescue League of Okemah (ARLO) was founded on November 20, 2015, in an effort to help the Okemah Animal Shelter place dogs and cats in homes rather than euthanize them. Prior to ARLO's founding, the city animal shelter would euthanize animals they found if they weren't claimed by their owners within 72 hours. There was no advertising. Pet owners were responsible for contacting the shelter. If pets weren't claimed, they were killed. That was that.

The founders of ARLO became aware of this crisis and formed a non-profit rescue group to help reunite the shelter animals with their owners. For those who weren't so fortunate—the strays and unwanted and unloved—ARLO stepped in.

Now dogs and cats that are impounded or lost/found are introduced to the public on ARLO's Facebook page. Foster homes and adoptive homes are found. Dogs and cats are examined by veterinarians, tested for heart worms (FYI it's as certain as death and taxes that a dog who is older than 6 months and is recovered by ARLO will be positive for heart worms), mange, vaccinated, and spayed/neutered. The members who are on Facebook will share posts. So will their friends. And their friends will share, too. An animal that might never be known to anyone, who is hiding away in the pound facing death, can now potentially reach hundreds of people. Hopefully, one of those people will reach out and take that animal. ARLO also networks with other rescue groups, sharing stories and photos, and often these other rescue groups locate forever homes for animals ARLO rescues.

Before Casey and I rescued each other, I had helped ARLO out financially here and there. But now, it really hit home with regards to what they are doing. Not only do they try to save dogs and cats from the pound, but they rescue strays, neglected, abandoned, and abused animals (including a starving donkey, which is a tragic story). And they worry about the strays they can't get their hands on, like my Casey.

I sent a message to my ARLO friend, Debbie, and asked her about the Facebook post that Ian had showed me. I asked her if Casey indeed belonged to this girl. Well, the girl to whom Casey *used* to belong.

Debbie sent me the best reply ever.

"NO!"

Casey had been roaming around Okemah for a few weeks. This girl was worried about him because she hadn't seen him in several days to give him some food. She would feed him when he came, around but he didn't stay with her.

And then Debbie sent me a message with words that I'll never forget.

"You're the only one he's stuck to."

Gulp. I had to stop and think about that. I still do. That little sentence still melts my heart. Seven words that still give me chills and fill my eyes with tears.

That's because God sent Casey to me. Or me to Casey. Or both, I think. And now I'm his mom. And he's my coonhound.

So, I posted my own Facebook story about finding Casey. On June 23, 2017, ARLO posted one, too, called "Casey's Happy Ending." I've archived it and here it is.

Back on June 4th this dog was posted when a woman found him and was looking for his owner. We shared him and promised to try to find a place for him if the owner was not located. In no time this fella moved on, she could not keep him secure.

Fast forward to June 21st and we are notified that this starving Hound dog is at a home in town and has a wound on his side. We have no place for him! But we do our thing and start trying to figure out a game plan. We just aren't having any luck. No room and the budget is tight. His luck was about to change. A friend and Supporter of ours took this boy in and named him Casey. She took him to the vet for vaccinations, neuter and stitching up the wound. He is heartworm positive and she will take care of that treatment too! She says, "He is here to stay. So he's all mine! Did I mention how sweet he is?" We are thrilled for this boy and couldn't be more Thankful for Ann stepping up to help him.

ARLO places animals in approved foster and adoptive homes. Even when money is scarce or non-existent, as it usually is, ARLO goes out of their way to save these animals. Saving a life might mean the dog has to spend some time being boarded at the vet until a foster home can be secured. ARLO also works with out-of-state rescues and transports dogs and cats to rendezvous with other rescues so the animals can find their forever homes. As of this writing, ARLO has saved over 800 lives!

My expertise has evolved into utilizing my truck as a dog transport to take puppies and dogs to meet other rescue groups, like Lucky Mutts from Wisconsin. I really enjoy this, and of course, I fall in love with at least one dog during the journey, and I always cry when they leave. I just do. I even splurged on a backseat cover from Duluth Trading Company to protect the leather backseat from dog crates, dog hair, dog nails, dog pee, dog poop and dog vomit.

FIX Okemah is a program started by ARLO in 2017. It is a low-cost spay/neuter program. For $25.00 (matched by ARLO), pet owners can get their dog or cat fixed as well as get their vaccinations. All the owner has to do is deliver the pet to the store owned by Misty, the ARLO treasurer, and ARLO does the rest. They load up the pets (dogs and cats are transported on different days), drive them to Checotah, Oklahoma, about an hour and a half away, unload them, wait for the surgeries, load them back up, drive back to Okemah, and return them to their owners.

One female dog can have two litters of puppies every year. If her litters average 6 puppies/litter, that's 12 puppies/year. If she had two litters/year for 10 years, that equals 120 puppies, who can also reproduce. The same goes for cats having kittens.

And male dogs? There's really no way to calculate how many puppies they can sire in 10 years, since they can impregnate many, many females. Hundreds, if not thousands.

To date, around 400 pets have been fixed because of ARLO. Thousands of puppies and kittens have been prevented. So, thank you, ARLO! Please spay and neuter your pets, if you haven't done so.

The city of Okemah passed a spay/neuter ordinance that took effect on November 1, 2019! Residents will have to pay a fine if their dogs are intact after November 1. To help low income/poverty-level families, ARLO reduced the price of FIX Okemah to $10. For truly dire circumstances, ARLO will step up and absorb the fee. It's not that we are flush with cash, we just don't want to be flush with puppies and kittens.

Money is *always* tight, even with discounts from local veterinarians for care and treatment. Donations (monetary as well as pet supplies, including dog/cat food, leashes, toys, crates, and beds) are always accepted, via PayPal or cash or checks mailed directly to ARLO (P.O. Box 214, Okemah, OK, 74859). Other fundraisers include:

- Pasta for Paws, a spaghetti dinner and silent auction at Christmas time
- Indian Taco dinner in August
- Raffles
- Various businesses in Okemah have "tip" jars for ARLO.
- Wish lists on Amazon Smile and Wal-Mart online shopping
- Angel Trees with wish lists at Christmas
- ARLO tee shirt and cap sales
- Garage sale in the summer
- Bake sales/adoption events
- A booth at Pioneer Day, Okemah's birthday celebration
- Halloween treat baskets for sale

- Valentine's Day treat baskets for sale

- Facebook $5.00 Fridays Fundraiser

- Special rates on adoptions

- Proceeds from sales of this book!

- More events as we think of them!

Volunteers do this. No one is paid a penny. ARLO has five to seven volunteer board members (one of them is yours truly, as of February 2019) and others who volunteer in different ways, according to their circumstances. Volunteers who help at fundraisers. Volunteers who send out pleas for money (we *all* do that). Volunteers who foster. Volunteers who adopt. Volunteers who drive dogs and cats to the vet. Volunteers who love their new fosters. Volunteers who cry when their fosters leave for adoptive homes. Volunteers who adopt their fosters. Volunteers who cry when an animal can't be saved.

How blessed is he who considers the helpless; the LORD will deliver him in a day of trouble.

Psalm 41:1

As I said, since I rescued Casey, I've stepped up my game. Not to brag. Not at all. But now I feel this is something I've been called to do. One new friend at church just asked me how long I have been in the animal rescue ministry. I love that! This *is* a ministry! Thank you, Dr. Hulson!

It's easy to write a check, or eat spaghetti at a fundraiser, or drop a few bucks in a tip jar. And if that's all someone can do, that's great. No complaints. ARLO needs that and appreciates each and every person who helps. And each and every penny.

Getting in the trenches is a different story. An eye-opener. There is a strong possibility that it becomes an "I hate people" experience. ARLO volunteers, like all animal rescuers, are in the trenches. Constantly.

I got my first chance to get down and dirty in the animal rescue trenches. Misty and I took bags of dog food to a very small town east of Okemah. The owner, who was confined to a wheel chair, couldn't afford to feed his mama dog, her 9 puppies, and another adult dog (possibly her sister).

These dogs were starving before our eyes. They had a "fenced" yard that a buffalo could go through. Their source of water, even though the house had plumbing (just no one who cared enough to spray water in a bucket), was a nasty pool of water that came out of a tin horn in a drainage ditch.

Surprisingly, the puppies didn't look like they were pit bull mixes. These puppies looked like collie and Australian or German shepherd and border collie, mixed together. Who knows?

There are so many pit bulls and pit bull mixes. And there are *so many* idiotic people who think they are tough because they have a pit bull, even though they don't know the first thing about caring for it, or any dog. These people perpetuate the problem of overpopulation of pit bulls and pit bull mixes. They feel that they must have litters and litters of pit bull puppies from their dogs.

Misty and I poured a bag of dog food in a line on the ground, like feeding cattle, and the dogs devoured it. All except for one little tri-colored puppy, who was immediately attacked by the adult dogs as well as the puppies. Her little back had open sores on it and was missing hair. It wasn't mange. The hair had been pulled out.

While the dogs were eating, Misty and I started getting out dog houses and beds from the back of my truck. A serious, subzero, cold front was headed our way so we wanted the dogs to have warm houses. There was a lean-to on the south side of the house, so we put the dog houses there and stuffed them with blankets and beds. At least the dogs will be blocked from the north wind.

After we got everything set up, the daughter informed us that she had made a "shelter" for the dogs and showed it to us. It consisted of a plastic tarp on the front porch that wouldn't protect anything from a breeze, much less a howling north wind. There was a little hay strewn in, but it would not work for one dog, much less 11.

Another attack on the little puppy occurred as we were setting up dog beds. Misty picked up the puppy, and she immediately sank into Misty's arms. Misty barked at the daughter to give the dogs some water, and we watched as she sprayed water (at least it was potable) into a… get ready… *skillet*.

In good conscience, I couldn't leave that puppy there another second. I started crying and told Misty I'd take her. David was going to kill me. I'll deal with that later. This puppy will be dead by tomorrow if I don't take her with me.

Misty told the owner we were taking the puppy and we'd be back for the others soon. He didn't want to let any of the males go. Of course not. You can't have 5,000 puppies without any males. The daughter asked if we were bringing the puppy back.

"NO!" Misty said.

We left bags of dog food, and the owner was instructed to feed the dogs. As we got in the truck and the puppy warmed up, I noticed how really cute she was. Aren't all puppies? As I stated earlier, she was tri-colored. She had a pink and black nose. I told Misty she looked like she was part border collie, and Misty agreed. This puppy needed a name that connotated beauty. Her nose made me think of an opal. Opal. My grandmother's name.

"Opal," I told Misty. "I'm going to call her Opal."

We drove back to Okemah. Opal snuggled in with Misty and then with me after I dropped off Misty at her store.

I took Opal over to Valerie's house. Valerie was there with Brett, Camden, and Cale. Opal played with the boys, although she couldn't roll over on her raw back. While we ate supper, she was quiet and observant.

When it was time to leave, Opal snuggled up in the passenger seat. I kept my hand on her and petted her the whole way home. Sound familiar?

Misty sent a crate with me, so when I got home, I set it up and put Opal in it. Casey and Ajax trotted over to investigate, and Opal barked at them. I told her to hush and she did. She didn't make another peep! I let her out and put her on a leash to take her out to do her business. I fed her and watched her as she quietly explored the living room and kitchen.

We keep a treat jar on the counter by the back door. Ajax is an expert, a true professional, when it comes to manipulating—I mean asking for—treats. I gave him one. I gave Opal one, too. Once was all it took. She kept going back to the "treat spot." Casey gets treats, too. However, he knows he'll get one, so most of the time, he stays in his dog bed and lets Ajax do all of the work.

I sat in my chair to watch TV for a while. There was a blanket on the floor by my feet, *my* blanket that has since been taken over by Casey. Opal curled up on it.

When it was time for bed, I tucked Opal in her crate. I put my blanket in there for her. She whined once, and I told her to hush. She did. And that was that for the night.

The next morning, she followed me into the bathroom so I could get dressed. David was in there, and she walked up to him. He bent down and petted her. Whew. He hadn't been too thrilled the night before, but the ice was melting. And he knew I was taking her to the vet for a few days for her shots and to get her back checked out.

When I got to the vet, I was inundated by four female vet techs. They all fell in love with Opal and scooped her up. I told them I needed to go get her a collar.

"Oh, we have collars over here!" one of them exclaimed.

I told them to go pick one out, and it was like I gave them a limitless Tiffany's credit card! They brought a couple of collars back for me to choose (my only stipulation was that it had to be pink). I told them to choose the collar, and after a few squeals of delight, they settled on one and snapped it around Opal's little neck. She was beautiful.

I kissed Opal good bye and went to work. Dr. Rosemarie Strong, the veterinarian, called me later and gave me an update on Opal's wounds. She would need a medicated bath for several days after coming home. But the kicker was, she told me one of the vet techs wanted to adopt Opal! I was thrilled. She wanted to take her home to meet her older dog and I agreed.

It was love at first sight, all around, and I'm happy to report that Opal has been adopted and is in a loving home with a new sister and mom.

I'm also happy to report that Misty and I went back a few weeks later and got the rest of the puppies and placed them in an amazing foster home with Paula, an ARLO volunteer. But instead of eight puppies, there were only seven puppies; another tri-colored one was gone. We looked and looked and had to assume a coyote got it. The daughter said there weren't any coyotes around, even though their ramshackle house was next to a pasture and woods. As I noted before, the "fence" was wire, but the wire was so stretched that anything, especially a puppy, could get through it. Misty and I watched two puppies climb through it and run around the pasture.

To date, all of the puppies have found loving, forever homes! Lucky Mutts found homes for six of the puppies. Another puppy was adopted through ARLO.

Finding homes, whether they are fosters or permanent adoptive homes, is one way that ARLO utilizes every single penny of donation dollars.

But not all of the dogs ARLO acquires come from the pound. Many are dumped. Healthy dogs. Unwanted dogs. Unloved dogs. Abused dogs.

And in case you need a couple of "I hate people" examples, I present to you Liberty and Jack Walker.

Liberty is a Great Pyrenees (melts my heart) with a badger face and tan markings. He was found by some good men from Liberty Oil in Okemah in July. Liberty was literally dying before their eyes. They called ARLO and Heather—a volunteer and former board member— went to get him. She was able to pick him up by herself because Liberty only weighed 24 pounds. Besides starving, he was severely dehydrated. Once she got him to the vet, they determined that Liberty was also infested with worms, including hook worms.

Who did this? Who dumped Liberty? Who neglected this sweet boy to the point of death by starvation?

All I can say—well, I can say a lot but it's not fit to print—is God bless the men at Liberty Oil who found this dog and called ARLO. God bless Heather for going to get him and taking him to the vet. God bless the vet. God bless people who have donated towards Liberty's vet bill.

The vet sent us updates regarding Liberty. Little by little he gained strength. He was treated for worms and after a couple of weeks, the vet sent a video of Liberty grabbing his food bowl and pulling it closer to him!

Liberty is now in an approved foster home with Laura, an ARLO volunteer. God bless the fosters!

Jack Walker is a Treeing Walker Coonhound. Yep. Just what this book is about. Gulp. He was discovered by Brince, a friend and supporter of ARLO, who was at home working in his yard (he lives in the country) and heard a dog whining and crying. He followed the sounds, cutting through thick brush to reach an empty, abandoned shed across the road from his house. Shut inside, without food or water, of course, was this poor coonhound whose back legs and rear end were torn up with wounds. Wounds which looked like bite marks. Multiple bite marks. *LOTS* of bite marks. Wounds which made me and a few others think that this poor dog was used as a bait dog.

A bait dog is one that is used to train dogs, mainly pit bulls, to fight. Usually, they are beagles or dogs that are very sweet in nature. Or dogs that are listed as "free to good home," where the owner will never check on their dog they gave away to a "good home." Most often, the bait dogs are killed by the fighting dogs. If they aren't killed, they are discarded, broken and bleeding and slashed to pieces, like a piece of trash. Left to die on their own. With absolutely no one to love them and help them.

Remember that special place in hell? It's getting more patrons.

Brince called Misty and he took this poor coonhound to the veterinarian in Seminole himself. God bless him. As I stared in horror at these photos, I kept thinking about what I would name this coonhound. See where I'm headed with this?

If you've watched the series *24*, then you'll know how much pain and torture Jack Bauer goes through. And I thought that since this poor dog has been tortured and left for dead, ARLO should name him Jack Bauer. The vet tech thought Jack Walker was a good name. Jack Walker it is.

I was hoping I could foster (read "keep him for the rest of his natural life") Jack. But I had an upcoming hip replacement surgery and month-long recovery.

I fostered a dog I rescued out of the pound (Okie Carl) for two weeks until I could meet his new mom from California in Albuquerque. During this time, Casey got *super*-possessive of me. Towards the end, though, Casey settled down and got better. But I don't think he misses Okie Carl. So, it was decided that we can't foster long-term. Maybe just for a night or two.

Back to Jack Walker. David said "NO" on fostering because it could become long-term.

But Jack Walker is a coonhound.

"NO."

But Jack Walker needs a home.

"NO."

But…

"NO!"

I sent ARLO some money to help with Jack Walker's boarding. I prayed and prayed that someone would step up to foster/adopt this sweet boy. Someone who will love him as much as I would. God answered those prayers and Jack Walker got an approved foster home!

> *Rescue me, O my God, out of the hand of the wicked, out of the grasp of the wrongdoer and ruthless man, for You are my hope.*
>
> **Psalm 71:4-5a**

A lack of foster parents and too many dogs in the pound are the reasons that ARLO wants to have its own facility. Unclaimed, unwanted, and unloved dogs (and cats) would be safe at our facility forever, or until families adopt them.

Another reason for having our own facility is the fact that the worst thing about being a rescue organization is that we cannot save every dog. We try. Oh, do we try! But a lack of space, a lack of money, and a lack of foster/adoptive families seem to be perpetually stacked against us. So sometimes, we have to say "No" to pound dogs. We also have to tell people who call and tell us they have a dog they need to "get rid of" that "No, we can't take them."

From the reactions of some people, you would think that we are Satan himself. The "owners" proceed to cuss at, scream, degrade and insult whoever answers the phone. Because all of a sudden, it's our fault that their dog is pregnant, or they're moving, or the dog is expensive, or they don't have time, or it's old, or sick, or this, or that. It would be so much easier for them to take responsibility for their dogs. But for them, it would be so much easier if they could dump their dogs out with us.

Ignorance. Apathy. Stupidity. Meanness. These are some of the things that ARLO deals with every day. Every. Single. Day. But we are the "bad guys." And this becomes disheartening, maddening, frustrating, and soul-sucking.

Sometimes, and we hate this more than anything, we get a dog that is too far gone to save. Maybe the dog has been feral too long and will not be rehabilitated into a good pet, because people failed him, and he has absolutely no reason to trust a human. Ever. This has happened, and it tears us apart. Maybe the dog is too far gone physically to resuscitate, so the poor dog dies or we have to have her euthanized. And we cry. Because people neglected her. Because people starved him. Because people discarded him. Because people failed her. And we are the ones who cry. We are the ones who love these dogs. We are the ones who fed these babies. We are the ones who retrieved them. We are the ones who tried to rescue these poor dogs. We are the ones who agonize over a dog that is unwanted and unloved. But we also know that in the brief time we had this dog, he knew a little bit about love, and died being loved.

Deliver those who are being taken away to death,
and those who are staggering to slaughter,
Oh hold them back.

Proverbs 24:11

But ARLO keeps going; somehow, we keep going. Because someone has to help these animals.

If we had our own facility, a sanctuary, we could host adoption events. We could have spaces for dogs to run and play and have a good life with food and fresh water and a soft bed in which to sleep. We could have meet-and-greets with prospective adoptive families. We could host education seminars and workshops. Elementary, middle school, and high school kids could take field trips to our sanctuary and learn how to care for and save animals, and how to prevent overpopulations of dogs and cats. Have your kid's birthday party at the sanctuary! Veterans could come hang out with dogs.

Dogs are good for the soul. Dogs are good for just about anything that ails you. They are healers, even if they are heelers.

So, you might be wondering what you can do to help. If you bought this book, you've already donated a little money to ARLO because a portion of the proceeds goes to ARLO. Donate more, if you can. Donate in honor or memory of a loved one or a pet. Foster or adopt a dog. Buy a collar or blanket or sack of dog food then call us at 918-623-6457 and see where you can bring the items. Instead of birthday or Christmas presents, ask people and family to donate to ARLO for you. You have enough stuff and it's going to end up marked $0.50 at an estate sale anyway, half-price on a Sunday. Volunteer at our events. Drive dogs and cats to the vet. Share our posts on Facebook, MeWe, Parler, and Instagram. Spread the word.

Find us at www.arlorescue.org. Check us out, and share this link to our website. Share our address: P.O. Box 214, Okemah, OK, 74859. If you order anything from Wal-Mart online, be sure and check out ARLO's Wish List and purchase an item or two for ARLO. If you order anything from Amazon, order your items on Amazon Smile and have a percentage of your order donated to ARLO. Facebook also has fundraisers, so have one for ARLO.

If you've done any of these things, thank you. From the bottom of our hearts, thank you!

And please pray! Pray for the ARLO volunteers. Pray that ARLO gets our own facility. Pray for the animals in need. Pray that they are found. Pray that they are rescued. Pray for God to use you in some way to help these animals. It will change your life, because it changes the lives of these animals.

Chapter 7

"No Dogs on the Couch"

When we moved to our house in September of 2016, we bought a new couch. I loved our old one: a big, brown leather couch. The seat on each end reclined. Sure, there was dirt and dog hair on it from Ajax and Lucy using it as their personal bed. Rascal had gotten too old to jump up on the couch and was afraid to jump down. He preferred Lucy's bed.

The couch was easy to clean and wiped off easily. That's good because little Lucy left a ton of white hair where ever she went. On our lap. On our clothes. On the couch. I'm surprised she wasn't bald. I've truly never seen a dog shed more than she did. She dropped hair like Charlie Brown's little Christmas tree dropped needles.

David thought we needed a sleeper sofa. We found a really nice brown, fake suede sofa with a queen-size sleeper in it. It wasn't cheap. And it wasn't going to be easy to clean. Therefore, the new rule in the Jayne household became <u>NO DOGS ON THE COUCH</u>. File that away for later.

God sent Casey to us on June 21, 2017. So far, with me as the main enforcer (yes, me the dog lover), dogs stayed off the couch. They were relegated to their poor, lumpy, Serta dog beds-of-nails.

David had recently had back surgery. On July 4, he didn't feel like going with me to watch the fireworks display at Frontier City, a nearby amusement park. Justin and Ian had gone to shoot off fireworks at the house of one of Justin's friends who lived in the country. So, it was just me going to watch fireworks. David was staying home with the dogs.

The great thing about this fireworks display was that I didn't have to actually go *in* the amusement park. I parked on the street behind it and got a great view of the beautiful fireworks. Then I simply drove home; no crowds or glommed-up parking lots.

The fireworks didn't last long. When I came home, guess who was stretched out on the couch? The *new* couch. The couch on which no dogs were allowed. *That* couch.

Hint: it wasn't David.

It was my dear, sweet Casey. It was at this moment that I learned that the only dog who sheds more than a beagle is a Treeing Walker Coonhound. Don't ever buy the line that "short-haired dogs don't shed."

"What is this?" I asked David, pointing to the tri-colored coonhound laying on our couch. The couch that, until this day, remained free from dog hair.

David looked at me and calmly said, "Casey was scared. He could hear fireworks. He calmed down when he got on the couch."

"Calm" meant snoring like a buzz saw. I walked over to Casey and he raised his right hind leg. He always does that submissive posture. It makes me smile and it makes me sad. Did Casey do this to the monster who used to have him, submitting to him, to no avail? I shudder to think.

Needless to say, July 4, 2017 marked the end of the "no dogs on the couch" rule. It was scrapped. Shredded. Annulled. Vetoed. Erased from history.

The next day, I bought an ugly brown sofa cover from Ross for $19.99. I covered up our beautiful couch with this thing and tried to make it look better with blue kilim pillows. It really didn't help, and soon the pillows became dusted with dog hair.

After several washings, I decided to splurge at Ross again. This time I bought a soft blue and white fleece blanket with a Moroccan-style pattern, also $19.99. I retired the ugly brown sofa cover (read threw it away). The blanket isn't bulky and can be washed easily. And it is. Frequently. With Melaleuca lavender detergent and about three squirts of Melaboost lavender laundry scent enhancer.

I also found a couple of beagle pillows at TJ Maxx, which now have dog hair on them. One of them, featuring a large beagle face wearing glasses, has a hole chewed in it by a certain Treeing Walker Coonhound. Sometimes, it is found throughout the house and I move it back to the couch. It's only that pillow. Casey leaves the others alone.

Now that Casey is allowed on the couch, he takes sheer delight in snuggling with whoever is on the couch with him. Snuggling quickly evolves into crawling halfway into your lap. Or, maybe, he will lie next to you with his head on your leg or pressed up against it. If one or both hands aren't on him somewhere, Casey will use his paws to swipe at you until your hands are caressing his ears, cheek, or sliding down his ribs and patting him. There must be a hand on him. He will also sit as close to you as possible, with one paw on your thigh.

And if you think for one minute that you'll have the couch to yourself, think again. With Casey's newfound perch, he can't wait to get up there alone or with company.

Once, Casey was in the dining room. I came from the kitchen into the living room to sit on the couch. As I was sitting down, this 60-pound coonhound ran, propelled himself, and leaped over the footstool, onto the couch with me! He looked like a reindeer. He promptly slid right next to me and pressed himself against me.

You can forget lying on the couch by yourself, too. Soon a coonhound will carefully crawl up on the couch and scooch between you and the back of the couch. Casey's head nestles right on your chest and his front paws flop onto your chest or belly. Nap time!

Treeing Walker Coonhound: They are primarily workers/ hunters that are a bit too anxious to lie idly around a suburban home or condo. (13)

Jumping off the couch is almost as much fun as turning into a coonhound rocket to jump on the couch with somebody. It involves a little more effort, but it is great as a shortcut, especially when it is time to eat.

Our living room and kitchen open up to each other. We have a pool table behind our couch. When it's supper time, and someone walks out on the patio to get the dog bowls, Casey creates a new exit off the couch. It involves leaping over the back of the couch onto the floor and racing to get the food.

In order to leap, though, Casey has to plant both front paws on the top of the couch cushions at the back of the couch. Then, his hind legs push off like a show jumper and there's an airborne coonhound for a split second. And our "new" couch? Well, now one of the back cushions has a nice rip in it from large coonhound feet. But it can be sewn back together. The blue blanket covers it up most of the time, except when we have company and move the dog hair-encrusted blanket. David eventually put his surgical skills to use and stitched up the hole.

On one of my forays into TJ Maxx, I found a plush, pink Pendleton blanket. This will be my blanket, I thought. One I can curl up with and watch TV. No dogs will be allowed on my blanket.

Go ahead. Laugh.

That lasted, for oh, about five minutes after I brought it home. If that long.

Casey likes to get in my reclining chair with me. It took me a while to figure out what he wanted. He comes up to the right side of my chair and paces around, sometimes barking a little. When I finally clue in and lower the chair a little, Casey hops up quickly. Sometimes he clambers up.

He likes to sit next to me or on my lap and press himself up against me. I mean *right up against me.* There's no room to swipe a credit card. And I love it.

To be picked out by a dog is an amazing thing. And to have a dog decide you are the one they want to sit with is an honor. Sometimes, while Casey is in my lap, I feel like I am going to burst with pride. Other times my eyes fill with tears because I love Casey so much. I imagine what his former life might have been like and I tell God thanks for sending this coonhound to me. I'm grateful to have him in my lap.

Besides pressing right against me, Casey has another ritual in my chair. First, he will lie across my lap, perpendicular to me (for math people) on his left side. He might rest his head on the arm of the chair, but most of the time I put my hand under his head and hold his front feet with both hands. That way I can pull him closer to me and give him kisses. I'll talk to him and he makes a little strained, wheezing sound, like he is talking back to me. Cuddling like this prompted Justin to tell me that I hold Casey like a baby. So? What's your point?

This is also a good position for Casey to be in so I can stroke his ears. They are longer than Ajax's ears, so I'll start at the top by his head and run my fingers down his ear. Over and over and over. Or I'll take an ear gently in my hand and twirl it through my fingers. It's very soothing for Casey. And for me.

After a while, Casey will shift positions and lie lengthwise over my legs. He will go to sleep and start to snore. Then after a while, he will wake up and roll over to my right side and lie lengthwise (parallel) next to me in the chair on his right side. If I don't scoot to the left fast enough, Casey rabbit kicks me with his back legs so I'll make some room for him. Then he's good to have a nice long snooze. And snore. Some nights I've slipped out of the chair and left him there.

I thank God that I have this 60-pound coonhound on my lap who knows he is safe and trusts me enough to fall asleep in my lap and snore. And fart. Nose-hair curling farts.

Don't get me wrong. I love it when Ajax is in my lap, too. I'm honored when he decides to jump up to be with me. But he's not a snuggler. Not at all. He's content to lie next to me and allow me to pet him. Little by little he stretches out and scoots over so I have to move my legs to the side. He has three-fourths of the chair to snooze away in while I stroke his velvety soft ears. After a while he will wake up and hop down to get in his dog bed or on the couch.

David did draw the line at dogs on the bed. Not long after Casey became a Jayne, David walked into our bedroom and yelled for me to come in there. I didn't know what was going on and prayed it wasn't some big, hairy spider in our house.

We have a zebra print comforter and lots of pillows piled up in front of the headboard (when the bed is made). For some miraculous reason, on this occasion, we had made our bed. Was company coming? Had boredom set in? Or the most likely reason: a moment of temporary insanity? I don't know.

There wasn't a big, hairy spider in our bedroom. There was a big, tri-colored coonhound sprawled across our bed, sphinx-style, looking at us and possibly surveying his new-found kingdom. I'm pretty sure he wagged his tail.

I thought it was adorable. My dog Rusty had slept with me before David and I got married. I had no problem with dogs on the bed.

David failed to see how cute it was. I'm sure he envisioned coonhound, and then beagle, hair all over the bed. David put his foot down on the "No dogs on the bed…ever" rule.

Casey, however, wasn't about to leave his newly-found haven. And we had our first introduction to the stubbornness of coonhounds. Calling him didn't work. Clapping our hands and snapping our fingers at him didn't work. We literally had to drag Casey off the bed.

As far as I know, Casey only got up on the bed a couple more times. I was on the bed, and he hopped right up with me, to my delight! So did Ajax. Then David walked in. The party's over, boys. Once again, Casey had to be dragged off the bed.

The second time was a secret between the boys, the dogs and me. I was on the bed, and Ian and Justin came in for something. Casey and Ajax took that as an invitation to join me. So did Ian and Justin. The dogs relished the attention because they are so deprived. And I simply wiped the dog hair off the sheets and comforter. They were on my side, not David's. No harm, no foul.

And the pink Pendleton blanket? Well, I've come home and found it in the study room by Casey's dog bed. Or on the floor between my chair and the front door. Or in my bedroom. It was the blanket I put in Opal's crate for one night so she could smell my scent and not whine. Now it is Casey's blanket.

For Christmas, Justin and Ian got me a blanket with Casey's photo on it! So now I have my own blanket. With dog hair on it. It is still mine, relatively speaking. It gets regular washings and, for the most part, stays in my chair. But it has been found throughout the house on different occasions.

I just smile as I pick up my blanket, or shirt, or house shoes, and put them back where they belong. They are my things with my smell on them. And Casey loves them. He wants to smell me while I'm gone. I'm sure in his other life he didn't have a blanket. And I doubt if he wanted anything that smelled like the monster who had him.

Dog hair can be swept off. Holes can be sewn up. Casey has earned his place on the couch. And his very own pink Pendleton blanket.

Chapter 8

Sticks

Casey was settled in nicely with our family. He got along splendidly with Ajax and never ever growled at Ajax. He never growled at anybody.

The handles on the outside of the patio doors that open into the kitchen or sun room are lever-style, opening the door when pressed down. So, it is easy to open a door, especially with your elbow when your hands are covered in dirt or holding a plate full of grilled food.

Or if you're a coonhound. It didn't take Casey long to figure out the doors. I don't know if he watched us (coonhounds are very intelligent), or if it happened by accident, but Casey learned how to open the outside doors.

Treeing Walker Coonhound: These dogs are intelligent and proficient. Training is accomplished with little trouble, as these dogs are able to learn from example. (14)

When he wants to come in, he stands on his hind legs and paws at the door handle until it opens. *Voila!* He's in the house now and not out in the "elements" because we don't want him to have any flashbacks from when he lived on the street.

In some respects, it is kind of handy. When the weather is really nice, the breeze blows in from the open door, and that is nice. (I need to teach Casey how to shut the door when he comes in.) Every morning at 01:30, Casey needs to go out. On nice evenings he would stay outside, usually long enough for me to get back into a nice sleep. Then here he comes, pawing the door handle until it opens. And I get to get up and close the door. Unless I don't hear him. To date, no wild animals have strolled into our house because I slept through Casey's entrance and left the door open.

The only way to keep Casey outside is to lock the door. We did that during the day when he needed some fresh air and sunshine. Casey had to be a…dog.

Life was rocking along for all of us. Nothing seemed to really bother Casey. Until the exterminator showed up.

It was probably August or September. I can't remember when exactly. What I do remember is that the dogs were outside because the house was being sprayed for bugs. I was in the kitchen and the exterminator walked in, wearing his khaki uniform and cap, spraying the floors with the wand.

Casey appeared from out of nowhere, jumping on the patio door. We actually have two doors, the one we use and the other one which can be opened if we have to move something big outside. The doors are big panes of glass framed with wood casing.

My coonhound was growling and slobbering and barking and pawing, trying to get in the back door. He looked like he was possessed. My very own coonhound Cujo.

"He's not going to come through that door, is he?" the exterminator asked me. He had a worried look on his face. I did, too, as I made sure the door was locked.

"No," I said, quickly praying that Casey wouldn't break through the door and kill the exterminator. Cruel irony at work…Sorry. I couldn't resist.

Casey wasn't finished. He kept at it until the man left. And then Casey ran to the gate to continue letting the exterminator know that this was HIS house and I was HIS mom! Don't come back!

I let Casey in, and he was as docile as a lamb. I began to wonder if the monster who owned him previously had worn some kind of work uniform. I told David and the boys, then kind of pushed it out of my mind.

Until someone wanted to play pool.

David's brother, Rusty, and his family were here visiting from Las Vegas. I was sitting in a chair. Rusty's kids—Andrew, Coco, and Timothy—had been loving around on Casey on the couch. The more the merrier equated to more hands petting Casey. I was talking to Cheryl, Rusty's wife. Ian, Andrew and Coco went outside. Casey was alone on the couch.

Justin and Timothy decided to play pool. They got two pool cues from the rack and walked past the couch to the pool table, which is behind the couch.

Casey began to growl. It was a low, menacing growl. A warning growl. A "don't do that" growl. It was a growl learned in self-defense.

I told the boys to put the cues down and back up. They did and Casey stopped growling. A few minutes, later they picked the pool cues back up, and Casey started growling again. He lifted his head this time and was starting to bare his teeth.

Once again, I told them to put down the cues. Sticks. Casey doesn't like sticks. Because Casey has probably been beaten with a stick of some kind. Pool cues are sticks. So are bug-spraying wands.

I led Casey back to our bedroom and shut the door so the boys could play pool. That solved the problem.

Later, in the fall, we had Justin's football team over for a team meal. Casey sat on the couch and held up his left paw, greeting each boy. I got the boys' attention and told them they needed to let me know when they were going to play pool because Casey didn't like sticks.

I told the story of rescuing Casey to Dre, one of Justin's teammates who can run like Secretariat. Dre gave me a big hug.

Casey was very interested in the food, and he and Ajax managed to stay outside with the team while they ate. And they got a few handouts. Casey even demonstrated his ability to open the door and go inside. Justin's friend Dylan was amazed. He asked Justin if Casey could read, too.

Little Lucy kept her distance because it was so noisy. A couple of boys (Hunter and Chandler) paid extra attention to her, sat next to her, and loved on her. Pretty soon, I put her in our bedroom away from the noise and chaos.

A few boys wanted to play pool and asked me if they could. Casey was outside but when he saw the boys picking up the sticks, he started barking. So, he had to go sit with some kids on the other side of the yard and be occupied with petting and handouts while the pool game was going on. Casey still kept a wary and watchful eye out, though.

I'm glad Hunter and Chandler focused their attention on Lucy because her health started deteriorating quickly. She began having trouble digesting her food and started throwing up undigested food. She stopped eating, and three days later Lucy threw up one final time. Undigested food from three days previously. She was as weak as she could be, so I scooped her up and began to cry. I knew what I had to do. It was an hour before our veterinarian clinic closed, so I had no time to tell Ian or Justin what was happening. Justin was at football practice, so I didn't even bother to text the coach to see if Justin could leave.

Lucy was as light as a feather, and I placed her carefully in the car. She wasn't moving much. Dr. Strong was so kind. She gave Lucy a sedative and left to give me time to talk to Lucy. To tell her I love her. To tell her I'm sorry that people had been so mean to her. To tell her I was grateful she at least knew love for a couple of years. To tell my little, frightened-of-everything lemon and white rescue beagle good-bye.

Dr. Strong came back in and gave Lucy the final dose of drugs. Lucy slipped away almost instantly. Through my tears I told this sweet little dog one more time that I loved her.

It was October 2, 2017. When I got home, I found out that Tom Petty had just died. I had been fortunate enough to see him in April when he kicked off his 40th Year Tour. His first concert of the tour was in Oklahoma City. So, I came home after putting my sweet little beagle to sleep and found out that one of my favorite singers had died. What a crappy day this turned out to be.

A few days later, I picked up Lucy's remains. They were in a tiny little urn with flowers on it. She is now next to Baloo and Rascal in a cabinet in our bedroom. I'm glad Lucy came into our lives. I hope she knows she was loved and that she is missed. I still think about her and wonder what kind of life she had before the rescue found her.

Beagles are happy dogs: happy to be hunting, happy to be home, happy to be with their people. This disposition explains only a part of the breed's tremendous popularity. (15)

I hope little Lucy had been happy the last year and a half of her life. I hope she had been happy with "her people" because we sure loved her.

Amidst our sadness, I still wondered (and I do to this day), what had happened to my poor coonhound before I found him? Why was he so wary and fearful of sticks? I shudder to think. Was he tied up and beaten? Was he beaten because he doesn't like loud noises, like thunder or guns? Was he beaten because he barked? Was he beaten for fun because he was owned by a cruel and sadistic monster? I don't know. My guess is "all of the above."

I really didn't need more proof, but I got it anyway. I took Casey for a walk one day and we were almost home. A work truck pulled up to our neighbor's house and a man got out. He wasn't carrying any kind of "stick" but he had on a cap and uniform. Casey stopped dead in his tracks. He began to growl, a low, guttural growl. I took a better hold of the leash and told him it was okay. Casey was on my left side and the man was to my right. Casey walked to my right side, stopped, stared, and growled at the man. He was between us. My heart melted. He was protecting me!

We continued walking. I reassured Casey that this man wasn't going to hurt him. Casey walked a little bit, then stopped and turned around to see where the man was. He did that until we got to our driveway.

Again, I wondered what had happened to Casey before we found each other. It's probably best that I don't know. My imagination fills me in. And if I knew who did what to my Casey, well, I'd be writing this book in jail.

I discovered and joined a delightful group on Facebook: Life With My Rescued Coonhound. Someone in this group posted to see how many people had issues with their coonhounds and swimming pool equipment, such as nets and brushes, which are on long poles because her dog, Jackson, goes ballistic when someone holds the pool brush pole upright. She said he goes crazy when she dips it in the water and lifts it out. Jackson gets to the point of panting, being anxious, and "beside himself." She works with a trainer, and they are trying to get this behavior to stop by redirecting it with cues and treats.

However, she began watching videos about how coonhounds are trained. She thinks that whoever owned him had a live or dead animal or decoy on a pole. This is used to train them to tree raccoons, and she said Jackson exhibited the exact coonhound behavior that she saw in the videos.

Jackson's mom said she hates seeing him like this. He gets all wound up, then is exhausted afterwards. But they have to start getting him to associate the pole with treats, and work on this with him each day until Jackson doesn't react to the pole.

So that might explain part of Casey's problem with "sticks" and poles. But I think his "training" went farther than that and involved physical pain and beatings. I'd bet my last dollar on it.

I got the call from David a few weeks later. Casey had bitten one of the guys who cleans our swimming pool. They are dog people. They have black mouth curs and hunt wild pigs with them. They're used to dogs.

But when they're in Casey's back yard, using pool skimmers, well, that's a different story. Pool skimmers are sticks. Big, long, metal sticks. Prior to this, Casey was in the living room one afternoon and could see David skimming the pool. Casey began to bark and growl. I told him it was Dad! He settled down, but that's how badly this poor sweet hound was affected.

Casey didn't attack the pool guy head on. He waited until the man was walking out the gate. Then Casey ran up behind him and nailed him on the hand.

I was terrified they'd report Casey and he'd be taken away from us. They assured us that wouldn't happen, and David treated the dog bite.

Casey didn't even like the pool guys standing on the other side of "his" gate. They'd talk to him, and I'd stand out there and try to reassure him. Casey firmly planted himself between me and the gate and the "bad men." Again, my heart melted a little when he did that.

One of David's patients, Angel, is an expert dog trainer, so we immediately called him. Angel came out to the house a few days later, another strange man in Casey's yard. We told Angel what happened and I told him about Casey standing between me and the pool guys. Angel put his hand over his heart, smiled, and bowed his head. He knew Casey was protecting me.

But there was work to be done.

Angel told us we need to pick a word to let Casey know he needs to stop a certain behavior. Casey's behavior was barking incessantly at strangers with sticks. We selected "Halt!"

Putting it to the test, Angel picked up a pool skimmer. Casey started barking. One of us yelled "Halt!" firmly. Casey eventually stopped and went into the dog house. Angel said that was great. Casey would still growl from inside the dog house, and when he came out and began to bark, we told him "Halt!" again.

Casey never ran at Angel. Angel said many dogs will feel threatened facing their foe, especially one holding something. The pool guys verified that. But, Angel said, when their backs are turned is when the dog makes his move. And that is exactly what Casey did, when they were walking through the gate with their back to him. When they were vulnerable.

From then on, we kept Casey on a leash and sat outside so he could see that they were harmless. We would tell him "Halt!" and the pool guys would come up to Casey and pet him and scratch his ears.

Then their schedules changed, and they could only come out while I was teaching yoga classes. So, we just left the dogs in the house. I shut the iron gate between the sun room and our bedroom so Casey couldn't crash through the windows. And I prayed he wouldn't crash through the back door in the kitchen. If I happen to be home, I take the dogs on a walk or stay inside with them.

Another problem developed with the woman who cleans our house every two weeks. All was well and good the first few times. I'd stick the dogs outside and that was that. But when she mopped the kitchen floor or around the pool table and Casey could see her, he went into attack mode like he did with the exterminator, lunging and snarling at the windows and door. Mops are sticks. (That gives me an excellent excuse not to mop. I don't want to traumatize my dog.)

Since I work all day when the house is cleaned, I take the dogs to doggy day care. Problem solved. The dogs get socialized, Gina doesn't have to worry about being attacked, and I don't have to worry about her being attacked.

I pray Casey doesn't remember too much about his past life. But ugly reminders, such as "sticks" pop up from time to time. Hopefully we've remediated as many of the reminders of his abuse as we can. If someone wants to play pool, we put Casey in our bedroom. He can sleep on one of the two dog beds in our room, or the one in the closet.

The only "stick" that hasn't bothered Casey has been the cane I used after my hip replacement in September of 2019. I honestly didn't even think about it bothering him. He never growled or shied away from it. I couldn't bend over for 12 weeks, so I used the cane to scratch Casey while he was lying down. It didn't seem to faze him one little bit. He trusted me completely!

After Angel made a few house calls to help Casey, we enrolled him in basic obedience training at Angel's dog training facility, K9 University. Casey learned—well, for a while—basic commands like "sit," "stay," and to come when called. He absolutely would not learn "down." I could pull down firmly, but not too hard, on the leash or gently tug on his front feet, say, "down," and he wouldn't budge. Not. At. All. I tried and tried. The dog trainer who was helping us told us not to worry about it.

Part of me thinks maybe that's one of the reasons Casey was beaten. Or he was beaten while he was laying down. Or he was beaten until he laid down. Or he was beaten while the monster yelled or screamed "DOWN!" That just absolutely breaks my heart. I have never enforced "down" with him again. Maybe I could try a different word, but I'm sure it's still a vulnerable position for Casey no matter what word I use. I just leave it alone and our life has carried on. No worries.

I wonder how the monster who abused Casey would like it if he or she was screamed at or had "DOWN" yelled at him/her by someone much bigger and stronger while being whacked painfully anywhere on their body with a "stick" of some sort. Would he or she remember a sweet coonhound who was subjected to this? Would he or she like to meet this sweet coonhound's Mama? I'm guessing the answer to all of these questions is "No."

Chapter 9

Coonhounds 101

As I mentioned, after I became Casey's mom, I found a delightful and wonderful Facebook group called "Life With My Rescued Coonhound." Members of this group (LWMRC) have all rescued one or two or four or more coonhounds of all breeds: Treeing Walker Coonhounds, Bluetick Coonhounds, Black and Tan Coonhounds, Redbone Coonhounds, American English Coonhounds (Redticks), Plott Hounds, American and English Foxhounds, oh and beagles, Basset hounds, and bloodhounds. We share photographs, daily stories, and stories about rescuing our "coonies," a term of endearment for our coonhounds.

We also share Gotcha Days, Crossing the Rainbow Bridge days, problems, and funny stories. Members ask questions about what to do about a certain behavior, which harnesses are best, what kind of dog food we feed our coonies, medical conditions, and so forth. We also ask for prayers when our coonie is sick or goes to heaven.

One coonhound in particular, Ingrid, a beautiful Black and Tan Coonhound, posted conversations with her mom as Ingrid's journey with cancer progressed. These conversations included enjoying Timbit Tuesday with her mom. (I found out that Timbits are basically donut holes from a chain of donut stores in the northeastern United States and Canada.) Their conversations were filled with sweetness, love, and lots of tears. We all mourned when Ingrid went to heaven.

This group never disappoints, never fails to lift up others, and doesn't judge.

Becoming the proud mother of a coonhound allowed me to witness things that I didn't realize had actual names, until I joined LWMRC. Coonhounds 101 began. School was in session, and I had automatically enrolled in it. I'm not auditing it; I'm living it.

Ever since Casey became a Jayne, I made sure he wasn't hungry. Let me rephrase that. Hounds are *always* hungry. Beagles, Basset hounds, coonhounds, it doesn't matter. I made sure that Casey never missed a meal. Put it that way.

Casey weighed 42 pounds when I took him to the vet for the first time. Treeing Walker Coonhounds are supposed to weigh 60-70 pounds.

For the first couple of months, I fed Casey twice per day. Two scoops of dog food each time. Mealtime became a cause for celebration for Casey. This involved Casey spinning around in circles, jumping up, jumping backwards, and jumping side to side. He'd be a great reining or cutting horse. Throw in a few happy yips and a big coonhound smile.

Every time. Every day. Even after he got up to, and slightly north of, his desired weight of 60 pounds. My heart melts and my eyes fill with tears to have a dog who is so very grateful to get to eat. I know he had been on the street for a while and ate whatever he could find. And I know the monster who had him didn't feed him enough.

Casey has never refused any kind of food, either. We give our dogs leftovers. (If you're rigid about not giving dogs "people" food, skip on down to the next paragraph.) French fries, old meat, leftovers from restaurants—including beans, lettuce and tomatoes from Mexican food— toast, it doesn't matter. Casey eats it. Ajax, however, will snub certain things, such as ketchup, olives, lettuce, and tomatoes. Casey *never* does. I shudder to think what that poor dog had to scrounge around and eat before he found me.

The dogs are fed outside. When we had Lucy, she ate her $3.00-a-can special dog food for her kidney problems separately, up on the pool steps, away from Ajax and Casey. They got kibble. And scraps from time to time.

The evening ritual of gathering up the dog bowls, putting food into them, and taking them to their respective al fresco dining areas took place every evening around 5:00 p.m. (And Casey got breakfast, as well, until he got to 60 pounds.)

Voila! The dinner dance was born. Around 5:00, Casey starts pacing around. Then he picks up the pace, literally. A bark is added in case whoever is feeding him isn't smart enough to know what time it is. No need to look at the clock. It's 5:00. Not 5:00 somewhere. It's 5:00 *here*!

In case canine assistance is needed (if the human isn't getting the food fast enough), shark bumps and counter surfing (see below) are incorporated into the dance, along with chopping (learn about this in Chapter 10).

When the meal is finally set down, after dancing, jumping and spinning all around the patio, the food is gobbled up, occasionally with time taken to chew some of it. This ritual will happen again in exactly 24 hours. Or maybe in 23-1/2 hours. Or maybe in 23 hours. When the dance begins prior to 5:00, if it's especially obnoxious, the designated hound feeder (Mom) might comply. If Mom is busy, the coonhound must wait. And then Mom worries that said coonhound might be reliving his days on the street, searching for some small morsel to eat. Coonhound Guilt sets in. Well, it does for Mom. No one else seems to be affected by it.

The dinner dance segues to the dance to indicate when it is time to go for a walk. In the spring and fall, we usually take walks around 3:30. If I have a yoga class to teach, sometimes the walks happen after supper.

Regardless of when they occur, the coonhound performs a dance to again inform the ignorant human that it is time for a walk around the neighborhood. Pacing, running, barking, and shark bumps (described in detail later in the chapter) are utilized in order to get Mom's attention. So are bounding around, spinning in circles, hopping up on hind legs, and leaping. Basically, the same moves performed at supper time, but on the other side of the house. One drastic measure is running over to the wall by the door with the leashes, jumping up on the leashes so they rattle, and then running back to Mom. Sometimes the dance is automatically engaged when Mom walks over to the key basket, which hangs by the leashes.

The dance is just the beginning, however. Casey pulls like a wild stallion with a regular leash. We got a training collar with stainless steel, dull-ended prongs that don't hurt the dog, but keep said dog from pulling human shoulders out of sockets. Getting that on a 60-pound dancing coonhound is exhausting. Casey sits, for about 30 seconds. Then it's rodeo time. And also asking-God-for-forgiveness time after wrangling and wrestling a coonhound and uttering certain words that should not be used around children or training a dog. Add to this that Ajax barks the entire time and dodges his head while I'm trying to put on his leash and training collar, and Casey is rearing, literally, to go, makes for Mom being tired before the walk even begins.

Opening the front door is like opening the starting gate at the Kentucky Derby. If my hands aren't wound through the loops on the leash, Secretariat and Seattle Slew are out the door and running down the driveway. A good little tug on the training collars helps.

Taking a coonhound and a beagle on a walk together is never, ever boring. Everything is sniffed (I would love to have a hound dog's sense of smell for just one day). Everything is peed on (with male dogs, that is).

Gopher holes must be dug in to make sure there aren't any gophers present. Once there was. As we were walking along, I saw one poke his head out of his hole. We were on the other side of the street and Ajax began sniffing. He followed his nose to the gopher hole and the serious digging commenced. He didn't get him, but Ajax and Casey had a great time digging for the gopher.

Here's a piece of advice: try to avoid taking your coonhound for a walk at dusk. I made that mistake. Once. That is the bewitching hour for these dogs because that's when night creatures, say like, oh, *raccoons*, start to appear. While we didn't see any on our walk, the entire walk was spent with Casey looking up at every tree and making sure it was inspected for the presence of *Procyon lotor*.

Another lesson in Coonhounds 101 is that they are the perfect height for just about anything. They can walk up to the couch or chair and you don't have to reach over to pet them. Or when you're walking and they are right beside you, you can reach down and your hand is instantly on the head of a coonhound. Likewise, they can stroll up to most any dining room table and use their snout to sniff out what is on your plate. Or put their head in your lap. Or take the bag of Cheetos out of your lap and run off with it (Casey did this). If they stand on their hind legs, you can get a nice coonhound hug. Or they can see what is going on at the kitchen counter and offer their assistance. Or get whatever food item is on the counter. How handy! Hence, I learned what counter-surfing is.

The dog food is kept in a container below the counter. The first time I pulled out the container and opened the lid, Casey must have thought he was in heaven. He shoved his head into the bin and munched away. Of course, I let him. Poor hungry boy. FYI, I still let him do this. I scooped out some food and put it into his bowl and Ajax's, which were on the counter. Casey immediately stood up on his hind legs and started sniffing his bowl, giving his tongue the side swipe to get any bits of kibble that fell on the counter.

And don't think counter-surfing is just for meal time. Anytime a coonhound takes a fancy to seeing what is on the counter to eat, all they have to do is stand up on their hind legs, put their front legs on the counter, and walk down the length of the counter, eating whatever is in their path. Or grabbing whatever they find—say a package of hamburger buns (no names will be mentioned)—and considering it their edible spoils and booty.

Not only do coonhounds have long legs with which to counter-surf, they also have tongues that are about one millimeter shorter than an anteater's, so they can run it along the counter and gather up what is there. Their tongues are wider, too, thereby ensuring they can cover a larger surface area on the counter. What exquisite engineering God did!

As my friends in LWMRC can attest, coonhounds are very good at counter-surfing. Many of them have been rewarded with a thawing roast, a whole pan of cornbread, a cooked roast, ham, green beans, bread, cake, and a pot of stew, unbeknownst to their moms and dads. Until it is too late. When it is time for supper.

"Where's that pan of cornbread?"

Burp.

When an empty pot or pan is discovered, or a roast is MIA, the coonhound (with the bulging stomach and gravy on the jowls) is automatically blamed. The nerve of some people.

One friend on LWMRC had a coonhound who could open their freezer. This resulted in the hound dog eating, within one hour, a frozen pizza, a frozen bag of corn, and a frozen roast. *FROZEN!* The wrappers were never discovered either. She said they now have a padlock on their freezer and posted a photo of it. There's "childproofing" and there's also "coonhound-proofing."

After the counter surfing has accomplished its mission, or the coonhound has been told to stop, shark bumps are next. Shark bumps are necessary to inform the human that the coonhound's meal is not being prepared quite fast enough. The snout is the perfect height to ram the average human thigh. Repeatedly. Mom, Dad, brother, sister, aunt, uncle, friend. It doesn't matter. Because the coonhound is absolutely *starving*.

Shark bumps are also an effective mechanism to let humans at the dinner table know that a coonhound is in close proximity and is being ignored. And starving. The perfect-height dog is now elbow-level. An appropriately-timed shark bump on the human arm that is lifting a fork or spoon, filled with, say, meat or beans, causes said arm to be "adjusted" enough to spill said food onto the floor, lap, or into the mouth of the awaiting coonhound. Touchdown!

Even if the human arm isn't hefting a forkful of food, shark bumps to the elbow or thigh alert the human to the presence of the coonhound. The *starving, neglected* coonhound.

A strategically placed coonhound head on the human thigh serves two purposes. One is to let the human look down into two huge, brown, marble eyes. Eyes that look like huge tears are about to pour forth, due to the extreme hunger of the coonhound (this trick works well when performed by beagles, too). The second purpose of the head on the thigh allows the thigh to become a reservoir for drool.

Casey has perfected shark bumps and drooling. If they were rated in degrees of testing, he would have a black belt.

Most dogs will curl up to sleep. Coonhounds invented the <u>coonie curl</u>. This involves wrapping the body in a tight circle, often tucking the nose under a back leg or tail. It allows the coonhound to curl up neatly into a ball, which comes in handy when the coonhound wants to fit into a dog bed that is five sizes too small. Or when the coonhound wants to snuggle with Mom or Dad or sleep on the couch (you can put several coonhounds on a couch when they're in little furry balls). Coonie curls also provide a phenomenal defense mechanism in that the coonhound quite possibly becomes deaf to any voice which might be telling the dog to move over or to go outside.

My very first experience with a coonie curl, although I didn't realize it at the time, was with Shiloh, a foxhound my friends Randy and Kerianne adopted from the animal shelter. Randy is a preacher so file this information away, too, like you did when I told you that no dogs were allowed on the couch.

Kerianne told me she came home one day and went in the backyard to see Shiloh. Kerianne looked for her and yelled for her, but couldn't find her. Fearing the worst, that Shiloh had escaped (Kerianne had witnessed Shiloh walking on *top* of their stockade fence), she turned around to get ready to search the neighborhood for her foxhound.

That's when she saw Shiloh. On the deck. In a coonie curl. In a flower pot. A flower pot that was probably barely over a foot in diameter. And apparently it had caused Shiloh to become deaf as she totally ignored Kerianne frantically calling for her.

When she showed me the pot, I couldn't believe that a large dog could fit in a tight space like that. And what possessed Shiloh to curl up in the pot in the first place? Who knows? Sometimes there's no rhyme or reason to a coonhound. And that's what makes them so interesting, fascinating, and endearing.

Casey's favorite place for a coonie curl is the little dog bed in our master closet. It was Lucy's, and she weighed 12 pounds, so there was plenty of room in it for her. However, Casey can curl up tightly in it, or hang his head out of it so he almost capsizes. It's perfect during thunderstorms. Or when Mom needs company getting dressed in the morning. Or when Casey just needs some alone time. Or when the couch, Mom's chair, or any of the other 500 dog beds scattered throughout the house just don't suffice.

People on LWMRC are always posting photos of their coonhounds in coonie curls. We are invited to rate them on a scale of 1-10. Most of them are 9s or 10s. A few need a little practice. But they're all coonie curls none the less. And they're adorable.

Coonhounds, while sometimes enjoying a quiet nap by themselves, aren't very familiar with, or flat out ignore, someone else's personal space. In Chapter 7, I told you about Casey's habits with me in my chair and joining whoever is on the couch. A coonhound head on the lap (which may or may not extend to two forelegs and a torso on the lap) can be quite comforting and warm.

However, it doesn't bode well when one has to turn the page on a book, write something, or text someone. The aforementioned head lifts up and places itself under the arm or hand of the human who has so thoughtlessly taken their hand or arm off the coonhound for a split second. Additionally, forelegs and paws can wrap around an arm and pull the arm down to its rightful place on the coonhound head or shoulder or ribs so the petting can continue.

The personal space invasion continues to the outside as well, whether it's a patio chair or lounger by the pool. Because the best thing on a hot day is a coonhound clambering up on the lounger with you.

And no invasion of personal space, uh, snuggling, is ever complete without a 60+ pound profile of a coonhound blocking the view of the television. Sometimes it is a sitting profile, whether on the lap or chair. Sometimes it is a full standing profile, with four legs, planted firmly on one's thighs, holding up 60 pounds of coonhound flesh. Sometimes, it isn't a coonhound profile but rather a full-frontal coonhound derriere right in your face. And for good measure, add a little gas-breaking. If the coonhound is facing you, there's likely to be a wet, ice-cold nose on your face somewhere. Or in your ear. Burps right in your face add a touch of elegance and atmosphere, too.

I don't know about other coonhounds, but Casey is not a big licker. I know other dogs who will lick you until your skin is raw. My niece Andrea had a little rescue mixed-breed who would lick you constantly and my friend from yoga, Suzy, has a border collie who will lick you until the cows come home. Casey's licks are confined to one lick to the nose, chin, or sometimes right across the mouth. Occasionally you'll get swiped two times with his large tongue, but never will you get a constant barrage of licks from him. The lick is usually a result of Casey hopping right up into your lap, and, as is the case with Mom, putting his face right in mine. His single lick to my face always results in a giggle from me. And a chill or two. And pride. I tell him thanks and that he's a sweet boy. And that I love him so.

The stubbornness of a coonhound can only be matched, and won, by a beagle. If they don't want to do something, like say, go outside since they've been inside for several hours, they will flat-out refuse. Until a treat is offered, that is.

Usually the request is totally and unashamedly ignored. Opening the door and calling to the dog, which rapidly escalates to a fish wife beckoning, can often go unheeded. Did my coonhound suddenly go deaf? No. Because he will hear the treat bag or jar rattle.

Sometimes, if I'm lucky, I'll get a sigh as a response. More often than not, I'll get the equivalent of a teenager's eye roll, which, by coonhound characteristics, is a side-eye. And in order to build up my dog-training esteem, to make me think that he is actually listening to me and *obeying* me, sometimes Casey will stand up. Then he will stretch, lie back down or walk towards another room.

If Casey is in my bedroom, and I'm trying to get him outside through the sun room, the above scenario is what takes place. There aren't any treats in our room, so I "win" by dragging him out by his collar, which is only achieved after I pull on his collar to try to get him out of his dog bed, which usually comes along with him for part of the journey. I pull up. He flops down. Then when Casey actually begins walking on his own, it's like he's walking to his doom. Once I've successfully gotten him outside, I have to lock the door and then make sure the other door is locked because he'll zoom over to it. On more than one occasion, the door has been unlocked and I have watched my dog open it to come right back inside the house. If only I could hold my bladder that long.

With all of this said, Casey has wrapped himself into a coonie curl in my heart forever. And he has convinced me that I will *always* have a coonhound in my life.

Chapter 10

"Gazelles That Bark!"

Coonhounds exhibit a wide array of barking, each one with a specific purpose.

"It's like having gazelles in the house that bark!"

A friend on LWMRC made that comment about owning coonhounds. She is spot on.

Remember I told you how Casey ran around the yard barking the first few days I had him? Yes, he was in a new place. Yes, there were tons of trees. Yes, raccoons and squirrels live in trees. Hence, they must be barked at, anytime of the day or night.

This deep, constant bark did come in handy at one point, however. It was in the form of an alert.

In Chapter 4, I mentioned that there was a really good story about Ajax. Well, here it is.

Ajax loves, loves, *loves* to go out in the front yard. All anyone has to say is "Front!" (the "F word" in our house) and he perks up his ears, races to the front door and waits to go out. Ajax has lived in three houses, and in all three of those houses, the front yard has always been a magical fantasy land for him. It's just adventure after adventure waiting to happen that beckons to him with some invisible, mystical power.

We had moved to our current house. Ian, Justin and I were in the front yard. Ajax and Lucy were with us. Lucy was on a leash because, even though she was scared of her own shadow, she would run away. Casey was on a leash, too. I had gotten home from teaching yoga classes. I had on a yoga top and pants and slip-on sandals. It was July. It was *hot!*

Some deer were between our house and our neighbor's house. Ajax would bark at them every now and then when he was in the backyard. For the most part, he either just watched them or ignored them completely. Until today. This hot, July day. This hot, July day when Mom was not wearing appropriate shoes for the woods, nor did she have her phone or a bottle of water with her.

Washington Irving, of *The Legend of Sleepy Hollow* fame, traveled through Edmond, Oklahoma, in 1832, with the Ellsworth Expedition. In fact, there is a marker east of town on the historic Route 66 (aka 2nd Street or Edmond Road) marking where he camped out.

Much of central Oklahoma and part of Kansas is delineated as "cross timbers." It is mostly comprised of post oaks and blackjack oaks, mixed with brush, other trees, grasses, and prairie. Settlers, pioneers, and explorers had to "cross" through this "timber" as they headed west.

Edmond has two elementary schools that are named after or reference Washington Irving. They are Washington Irving Elementary School and Cross Timbers Elementary School.

"I shall not easily forget the mortal toil, and the vexations of flesh and spirit, that we underwent occasionally, in our wanderings through the Cross Timber. It was like struggling through forests of cast iron."

Washington Irving

I, too, shall not easily forget the mortal toil and vexations of my flesh and spirit. Because the deer took off, and Ajax decided he would chase them. I took off after Ajax, forgetting that I absolutely hate to run. I yelled at the boys to put Casey and Lucy in the backyard.

Left alone in an inadequately fenced yard, or allowed to run off leash, a Beagle can disappear swiftly and stay away for hours. (16)

The deer and Ajax streaked off through our neighbor's unfenced yard. I saw white tails, including the one on a screaming, howling beagle. Then they were gone.

Our yard backs up to undeveloped property. I followed as fast as I could. There were many deer trails in the woods and brush. Panicked deer chased by a crazy beagle don't stay on the beaten path, though. They were headed east, as far as I could tell by Ajax's barking and yodeling.

I was yelling for him at the top of my lungs. More often than not, there were lots of thorny branches and vines I had to step through or go around. And since it was the height of summer, everything was leafed out. Snakes were out, too.

As I cut through the woods in my slip-on sandals, I began to pray that Ajax would turn around and come back. To the north was 15th Street, to the east was Air Depot Road, and to the west was the access road by I-35. If Ajax made it to one of those streets, he could easily get run over. I prayed, asking God to let my silly beagle come home. I also asked Him to please not let me step on a snake.

Ajax's voice was getting farther and farther away. I knew I had to hurry home and get the car to drive down 15th Street to Air Depot Road. I turned around and headed back the way I had come. I did notice a very cool, huge oak tree. I'll have to come back and look at it later.

What does all of this have to do with barking? Well, Casey was in the backyard. I could hear his deep voice barking a constant alert, a calling for Mom, or telling Ajax to get his butt back home. Regardless, I followed it until I was home. I got my keys and phone and took off. Justin said he would drive through the neighborhood and Ian said he would wait at home to see if Ajax returned.

I drove down 15th Street (a very busy street with several neighborhoods and which dead ends at Arcadia Lake). I stopped periodically and yelled for Ajax. I drove through a neighborhood northeast of our addition and yelled for him. Nothing.

As I drove along, I began to itch. I looked down and saw no less than a million chiggers crawling around on my arms and pants. Great. I brushed them off as best as I could and knew I had to wash them off before I was eaten alive.

David was on his way home from work when we passed each other. I slowed down and told him to keep looking as I had to try and wash off the gazillion bugs crawling all over me.

Once I got home, I raced into the bathroom, hopped in the shower and scrubbed myself quickly. I put on jeans, a long-sleeved shirt and boots. Because it's July.

Ian went with me back into the woods. He had put on jeans and a long-sleeve shirt, too. And he had a bottle of water and his phone. We took off where I had gone previously.

Casey was barking steadily, calling to Ajax. Or me. Casey kept me grounded and oriented. He was my homing device. Ian and I got to the place where I had turned around. Up ahead I could see a drop off, and I prayed Ajax hadn't fallen to his death.

Just then, Justin called Ian and said Ajax was home!

Thank You, God! And thanks for not letting me or my naked toes encounter any snakes.

Ian and I walked back to the house. Now we had a little bit of time to notice the woods and I showed him the big oak tree.

We followed Casey's deep bark and emerged back in our neighbor's yard, following the perimeter of it until we were in our yard. Their yard is almost like a meadow. Deer ran through it when they heard me shake the bucket of corn I fed them each evening. And once, I got to watch a pair of huge bucks fight during rut. I had time to grab my camera, stood behind one of the neighbor's trees and watched and clicked away on the camera. Technically I was trespassing, but the owner was out there watching with me. Now, they have thoughtlessly fenced their yard so their three little kids don't wander off. And it effectively put an end to neighborhood buck-fighting watch parties.

But thank God Ajax (or "YoYo" as David has named him) found his way home safely and unscathed. Again, like the midnight excursion in the dead of winter, a beagle cam would have provided some interesting footage.

I, on the other hand, did not remain unscathed. I took another shower and scrubbed my hair. And watched as chigger bite after chigger bite emerged on my legs and arms. I tried everything, including clear nail polish on the bites. These things lasted over two weeks, possibly because I'm on blood thinners. I don't know. I toughed it out during the day and popped Benadryl at night.

Needless to say, Ajax lost his off-leash privileges in the front yard for a very long time. And Casey has never been allowed off-leash at all, except in the backyard.

I've always known that dogs have different barks for different things. Dog people know this. Personally, I think coonhounds have their very own *specific* canine language.

Casey's morning routine involves running to the west side of the yard and running around the perimeter of the yard, sniffing for whatever creature dared to enter his yard during the night. Barking at the critter who left its scent in Casey's yard is a vital and necessary part of the morning patrol. The barking is only interrupted by some serious sniffing, but the barking can also be incorporated into the sniffing.

Patrolling the yard is for the owner's own protection. It is also an extension of the hunt. Once a scent is detected, it is imperative that the world knows that the coonhound is doing his job.

But it's not just a bark. It's chopping. Chopping is used when treeing raccoons to let the owner know where the dogs are and where they have treed the raccoon since a coonhound on the hunt can run at the speed of sound. Chopping is the equivalent to a four-year-old saying, "Mom!Mom!Mom!" Get it?

Chopping can take place at the base of a tree, whether the coonhound is standing on all fours, or hindlegs with the forelegs planted firmly on the tree. Chopping can also occur in the kitchen when the human isn't getting the coonhound's supper ready fast enough. The constant and repeated barking will continue to let the human know that (a) the hound is present, (b) the hound is starving, and (c) to *HURRY UP!* Combine the chopping with a shark bump repeatedly hitting the thigh and you know what it is like every night preparing Casey's supper.

Letting the human know that it is time for a walk is also a good time to chop. Chopping can be performed alone or during the go-for-a-walk dance for added flair and panache. It's important to chop while the leash is being snapped onto the dancing coonhound. And it's even more important to chop when your mom is snapping the leash on your beagle brother—chopping right in her ear for the ultimate effectiveness. Repeated screams of "HALT!" more or less go unheeded. The chopping continues when the front door doesn't magically open for the walk, and also as the coonhound bolts out the door. It persists while Mom attempts to lock the house while holding the leash of an exuberant coonhound, which can equate to holding the lead rope on a wild stallion.

Chopping was mentioned recently while I was watching the National Dog Show. Of course, it was when the Hound Group was being shown; specifically, the Treeing Walker Coonhound, which was recognized by the AKC in 2012. Amen.

Baying is another form of coonhound communication, usually involved in patrolling and picking up a scent. A bay's purpose is to alert the rest of the pack as well as the humans that a scent or animal is detected. Sometimes it's fun to just stand in the yard and bay for the listening pleasure of anyone, especially the neighbors. It is extremely useful when the coonhound is outside and has spied the human inside (who may or may not be in stealth mode when walking by the door or window). Baying lets the thoughtless human know that it is time for the coonhound to come inside. It can also be used to call to other dogs, as well as to alert the humans that a stranger is at the front door, or in the driveway, or in the neighbor's driveway, or walking down the street.

A bay is not a bark and it's not a solid howl; rather, it is like a short yodeling howl. A bay is an "AROOOO" sound. It can be rather high-pitched. The human version might be the sound a preteen male makes when his voice is starting to change. Magnify that sound about 30 decibels.

When a bay is used in the aforementioned scenario of wanting to come inside, it can be quite mournful, eliciting rivers of guilt to course through the human veins. Well, the mother's veins, anyway.

I absolutely *love* to hear a hound bay.

Baying can also be used to manipulate a coonhound into Mom's lap. Casey and Ajax both enjoy getting in my chair with me. When Casey wants in my lap and Ajax is already there, sometimes he jumps up into the chair with us anyway. Ajax growls and more often than not, he'll hop down. There's plenty of room (for the dogs) and I always feel bad when Ajax leaves my chair and has to suffer in his Serta dog bed or on the couch.

When Casey is not in the mood to share my lap with Ajax at all, he goes to the dining room window or front door and starts to whine. Then he will bay. Ajax gets fired up and whines, knowing those feral cats that I feed are out there. He hops down and zips over to investigate. As Ajax is running to the window, Casey heads back to my chair, deftly jumps up in my lap, and that is that. It happens repeatedly and poor little Ajax falls for it every single time.

Whether or not Casey is trying to get in my lap, indoor baying is useful to let everyone in the house know that the feral cats are outside. Just in case we didn't realize it.

Or that raccoons are fumbling around in the attic.

Yep. We had raccoons in our attic. We own a coonhound. The irony here is so thick you could cut it with a knife.

We could hear them running across the floor of the attic at night in our bedroom and living room. One of my friends in yoga told me that he had a friend who had raccoons in her attic. One night they fell through her ceiling and landed in her bed! They attacked her and her dogs, and she had to get rabies shots. I think raccoons are cute, but when I heard them running around, I prayed they wouldn't land in bed with me.

One night, David and I were watching television. Casey was in my lap and Ajax was in his bed. Raccoons tumbled and rumbled and fumbled across the attic space above the living room ceiling. Ajax exploded and Casey turned inside out as he spun off my lap. Baying, barking, and howling ensued.

David called our insurance company the next day, the insurance company we have had for more than 30 years, to whom we have paid premiums faithfully each month.

They don't cover raccoon damage.

Raccoons can chew through the wiring and cause the house to catch fire. So, if our house burned down because of raccoons, we don't get one dime from the insurance company. Same story with squirrels, mice, birds, vermin, and insects. The only animal damage our company would pay for is damage caused by deer. And bears.

I feed lots of deer, but we seem to be fresh out of bears. I thought about gathering deer poop and putting it in the attic. Or blaming it on Santa Claus' reindeer. And when I found out that it was going to cost $15,000 to exterminate, decontaminate, and repair the attic (all new insulation because our insulation was soaked in raccoon urine and feces and a decayed animal the wildlife exterminators couldn't identify), I began to consider making everyone a coonskin cap for Christmas. Suddenly raccoons weren't too cute.

We were able to negotiate a lower price (Happy Anniversary, Happy Birthday, Staycation, and Merry Christmas), and the Jayne household was raccoon-free. The clever little devils—and they are clever—had gotten in the attic by climbing up holly trees and scratching through two soffits on the east and west sides of the house. The holly trees had been planted by the people who built our house. They planted holly bushes and holly trees *everywhere*. Once we had the soffits replaced, those holly trees were cut down. And we switched insurance companies.

To Casey's credit, the soffits on the north side of the house (in the back yard) were unscathed. I guess a coonhound in the backyard is effective against raccoons after all.

While chopping and baying are serious business to a coonhound, so is the defense bark. It is a loud and angry chopping/what-are-you-doing-in-my-yard protective bark. It is useful to utilize when the neighbors are having their yard mowed and the mowers have dared to get too close to the coonhound's yard. It is almost a frenzy. And it's not complete without running up and down the fence doing the best Cujo impression a coonhound can do. Sometimes slobber and drool and frothing are effective enhancers.

Doorbells are a great way to illicit the defense bark. The coonhound will always beat you to the door because your life is at stake, and the coonhound is going to save you from the mailman or Amazon delivery person or the band kid selling pecans. If it's someone I don't know, I'll let Casey do his rabid, defense bark. I may or may not answer the door.

Sometimes there is no need for a doorbell or even a knock at the door. It might just take something as simple as looking in the front door, even if the person is Randy, our preacher.

When Ian was leaving to start his master's degree at Georgetown in the fall of 2018, we had a going-away party for him. It was late July, so the party was both inside and outside. David and I were inside waiting for more guests. Casey and Ajax were doing well with all of the people because they were getting treats.

Finally, Casey had had enough and headed to his dog bed in the study room for a little peace and quiet. Naturally, there is a dog bed in the study room, just like there is in basically every room of the house.

You know how when you go to a party, you're always confused about whether to ring the doorbell or just go on in? Or is that just me? Anyway, Randy and Kerianne (Shiloh's parents) arrived just as Casey was walking to the study.

Our front door is solid wood on the bottom half and the top half is paned glass. Randy put his face up to one of the panes of glass on the front door and blocked the glare with his hands, checking to see if we were in the house or outside. However, he forgot to check for a loaded coonhound.

Casey was on his back legs in a flash, defending his house against this invasive preacher. Of course, it was the rabid, slobbering, scary bark. All I can say is, thank God there was a door between Casey and Randy.

I'm pretty sure you go straight to hell if your dog attacks a preacher.

Randy jerked his head back, and David and I grabbed Casey and pulled him off the door, telling him to be quiet. To "HALT!" We were mortified. David held onto Casey's collar while I opened the door. Randy and Kerianne came in. Hesitantly.

Casey sniffed them, and they petted him, and then Casey was fine. We put him in the study and shut the doors. Casey was fine. No one was going to kill us. He had done his job. The preacher is alive and I am safe from the fires of hell for now.

Along the lines of barking, whether it is chopping, being on the alert, or defense, Casey has one particular bark. It's a single bark. A single, loud, sharp bark. Occasionally it is used when we are watching television and Casey needs to suddenly go outside. Right now. He will go to the back door and, during the most intense part of a show, he will bark once. It's equivalent to a human yelling, "HEY!" Forget that we've tried to get him to go outside for the last hour-and-a-half.

Mostly, though, this lone bark is reserved specifically for 01:30 every morning when Casey needs to go outside. Never mind that at 10:00 or 11:00 p.m. I have tried to get him to go out. Casey usually isn't having any of it.

But at 01:30 if I don't hear him come into the bedroom, he lets out the one, loud bark. Because he has to go outside. *NOW!* And I automatically know what time it is without looking at the clock.

When he's ready to come back in, he will open the door or bark a couple of times. When I let him in, he stops so I will pet him. Then he trots back to the living room to go back to sleep or piles up in one of the dog beds by my side of the bed, where Ajax is. But he must be petted first!

Did you know that coonhounds sing? Oh sure, some people might call it howling. I prefer singing. Howling is for sirens. Or the moon.

Casey will sing on command. One of my great delights is starting a low human howl and then letting it get higher. Casey can't resist. He sings back, often for minutes at a time. It can be mixed with some barks and bays, too. We can be at home or in the car. Casey doesn't care. He will sing.

Ian, Justin and I love to put our hands on his throat and feel the vibrations. Casey throws his head up, almost backwards, and lets loose.

Casey's singing is also a greeting and farewell. When I leave for work, I get a song. When I come home, I get a song. A duet, actually as Ajax chimes in. I have so many videos of my hounds singing to me on my phone. I've shared many of them on Facebook and of course on LWMRC. I so enjoy watching the videos later. Over and over again.

Having Casey sing to me makes me so proud. I am honored that he tells me hello and goodbye.

There's nothing like a hound dog song. To me, it is one of the most beautiful sounds in the world, besides a horse nickering, a soft, rolling thunder, and a gentle or mighty wind. It's hauntingly beautiful. I. Love. It.

Chapter 11

Coonhound Names

A good name is to be more desired than great wealth...

Proverbs 22:1

David has always said that Basset hounds can never have normal names. I believe that extends to hounds in general, and after being a member of LWMRC and Coonhound and Company groups on Facebook, as well as Coonhounds of Instagram, I definitely believe that this is true.

Many of these coonies are often-featured by their parents in these groups. And once we get familiar with these hounds, the names magically fit. Without even looking at who is posting what, I have been able to automatically identify, in alphabetical order, because there are no favorites: Captain Butler (his name truly fits this regal hound), Gambit (Mom is a phenomenal photographer), and Honeybug (famous for her side-eye). I am beginning to feel like these hounds are part of my extended family.

This list, which continues to grow every time I check in on these groups, is perfect for naming your coonhound. It can rival the books about naming your children, in my humble opinion.

There are variations of names as well as spellings. Nicknames are in parentheses next to the name. You might laugh out loud at some of the names or nicknames. Some owners who have multiple hounds, or have had a succession of hounds, name them with something in common, such as alcoholic beverages, famous detectives, superheroes, musicians, or athletes. I didn't include these names together since I let the computer alphabetize everything!

One particular family consists of seven blue tick coonhounds! They are littermates and affectionately called the B-Boys! I need to include all of their names here, even though they are scattered in the list of names below. The B-Boys are: Barnaby, Bastian, Bedrich (BedBed), Benedict, Bishop, Bixby, and Bronson.

Another litter of coonhound puppies and their mama were named after candy bars.

Some owners have the dog's best interest in mind if the hounds were particularly traumatized and keep the names the rescue gives them.

Grab a pen or highlighter and find your favorite names. There is space for notes. You might just find the perfect name, or come up with one of your own, after you get your first (or 40th) hound!

- Abbie (Abra Ka Dabra)
- Abby
- Abby Do
- Acai
- Achmed
- Addie Lee

- Addison
- Addy
- Aero
- Agrippa (Rip)
- Albie
- Albus Dumbledore
- Amie
- Angel
- Angel Dancer
- Angus
- Anne-Caroline (Annie-Bananie, Annie-Banoo, Annie-Bansters)
- Annie
- Anya
- Apple
- Aprilia
- Archie (Archibald)
- Arlo
- Artemis
- Aspen
- Astin
- Aston Martin
- Até (goddess of mischief)
- Athena
- Atlas

- Atticus
- Aubree Rose
- Autumn
- Avery
- Bailey
- Baldrick
- Baloo
- Bambi
- Bandit
- Banjo
- Barkley
- Barley
- Barnaby
- Barry McBarksalot
- Basil
- Bastian
- Baxter
- Bayou Huntress (Tress)
- Beans
- Beau
- Beau Beignet
- Beau Bennett
- Beauregard Justin Matisse
- Beckley

- Bedrich (BedBed)
- Beignet
- Bella
- Bella Boo
- Belle
- Bellow
- Benedict
- Bessie
- Betty Lou
- Biggie Smalls (Biggs, Mr. Bigs, Biggerton, Biggles, Dumbass)
- Bigglesworth
- Big Zee
- Bijou
- Billy Jack
- Billy Jack's One Tin Soldier
- Bingley
- Birdie
- Bishop
- Bixby
- Blair
- Blaster
- Bleu Cheese (Cheesy)
- Blithe
- Blu

- Blue
- Blueberry
- Bo
- Bob
- Bocephus
- Bodhi
- Bogey
- Bonesy
- Bonnie
- Bonzo
- Boo
- Booker
- Books (Bookie Boo)
- Boomer
- Boone
- Booty
- Boris
- Bota
- Bowie (Bo, Bowie Dog, Mr. Bojaynegles)
- Boze
- Brady
- Braun
- Bristol Sue
- Brody

- Bronson
- Bruce
- Bruce Springsteen
- Bruce Wayne
- Bubba
- Bucket
- Bucky
- Buddy
- Buddy Bones
- Bud Lightsey
- Buford T. Justice
- Bullet
- Bumpus
- Bunk
- Buster
- Butter
- Butterfinger
- Cabela
- Calgary
- Calhoun
- Callie
- Cami JB Jones
- Canada
- Candace

- Cane
- Captain Butler
- Carob
- Carver
- Casey (Case, Casey Dog, Casey Jayne, Special)
- Cash
- Cayanne
- Cayman
- Ceelo
- Cera
- Cersei
- Chance
- Chaos
- Charlie
- Charlie Coon
- Charlie Girl
- Chase
- Cheeto
- Chewy
- Chi
- ChiChi
- Chicken Nugget
- Chief
- Chloe

- Chrissie
- Chuck
- Chuckypants
- Cindy Lou (Lulu, PIA-pain in ass, Whosagoodgirl)
- Cinnamon Sally
- Clancy
- Clancy Wayne Hudson
- Clarence
- Clark Kent
- Clayton
- Cleadus
- Clementine (Lemon)
- Clifford
- Clooney
- Clyde
- Coco
- Coco Channel Mademoiselle (Coco Banana)
- Coconut
- Coe
- Coker
- Cole
- Coltrane
- Columbo
- Contrary Mary Jane

- Cooper
- Cooper Jughead Jones
- Cooter (Coot, Cooty)
- Copper
- Cora
- Cormac
- Cricket
- Curtis Lowe
- Daisie
- Daisy
- Daisy Lou
- Daisy Mae Clampette
- Dakota
- Dale
- Dalton
- Dan
- Danny
- Daphne
- Darla
- Darnell
- Daryl
- Dashing Daryl
- Deacon Blue
- Dempsey

- Deuce
- Dexter
- Dick
- Diesel
- Dillon
- Dingo
- Dipper
- Dixie
- Dixie Doodle Bug
- Dobie
- Dobrik
- Doc
- Dodger
- Dolly
- Dory
- Dottie
- Duc
- Ducati
- Dugan
- Duke
- Dynamite Dan
- Edgar
- Eleanor Rose
- Elektra

- Ella
- Ellie
- Elliebells
- Ellie Mae
- Ellie May
- Elliot
- Elvis
- Elwood
- Ember
- Emmi
- Emmylou
- Ernie
- Eros
- Esmerelda
- Eva
- Ezra
- Ezra Hound
- Fargo
- Faye
- FedEx
- Fern
- Ferris
- Finch
- Finn

- Finnegan
- Flint
- Flipp
- Flower
- Floyd (Moochy Von Moochenstein)
- Ford
- Frank
- Frankie
- Frannie
- Freddie
- Freddie Mac (Fredrick MacPoophead)
- Fresa
- Freya
- Freyja
- Frida
- Frisco
- Fuller
- Gaia
- Gallagher
- Gambit
- Gatlin
- Gemma
- General
- General Duke Whitehead

- General Stonewall Jackson (Jackson)
- Geno
- Georgia
- Georgia Mae
- Georgia On My Mind
- Georgie
- Georgie Girl
- Gertie
- Gilly
- Ginger
- Ginger Lou
- Ginger-Lu
- Ginny
- Gordy Howl
- Gran Dame Moonshine
- Grayson Kelly Campbell
- Green Arrow
- Gretchen
- Gretel
- Griffin
- Grover
- Guest
- Guinness
- Gumbo

- Gunnar
- Gypsy
- Gypsy Rose
- Hailey
- Hamilton Norbert (Hammy Norbert)
- Hammer
- Hank
- Hank Williams
- Hannah
- Hannah Banana
- Hansel
- Harley
- Harold James
- Harper
- Harriett
- Harry
- Harry Church Hound
- Harry Plotter
- Harry Potter the Hound
- Harvey
- Hatchet
- Hawkeye
- Hayden
- Hazel

- Heart
- Heath
- Heidi
- Henley
- Herb
- Herschel
- Hetty
- Hobbes
- Hobbs
- Hobo
- Holden
- Holmes
- Honeybug
- Honey Girl
- Hook
- Hooker
- Horace Waylon
- Houdini
- Houndy McHounderson
- Howie
- Huckleberry
- Hudson
- Hudson Blue
- Hundred Dollar Bill (Bill)

- Hutch
- Icarius (Ike)
- Indiana (Indy)
- Indigo
- Ingrid
- Ink
- Inspector Gadget
- Irish
- Irving
- Izzy
- Jacee
- Jack
- Jackson
- Jack Walker
- Jacob
- Jade
- Jake
- Jamie
- Jasper
- Jed
- Jemma Grace
- Jesse
- Jessie Lynn
- Jethro

- Jim
- Jinj
- Joebe
- Johnny Cash
- Johnny Walker
- Josie
- Josie Mae
- Journey
- Journie
- Jubel
- Jules
- Julie
- June
- Junie
- Juno
- Justice
- Kaboom
- Kacie
- Kaiser
- Kara
- Kelso
- Kentucky
- Killian
- Kipi

- Kit Kat
- Kolsch
- Kopa
- Kora
- Kouper Boop
- Lacey
- Lachlan
- Ladybird
- Ladybug
- Lafayette
- Larry
- Larry Bird
- Layla
- Layna
- Lee
- Leena
- Leonard
- Leopold
- Letterman
- Lil' Anne
- Lil' Blu
- Lilah
- Lilo
- Lily

- Lily Bean
- Lily Lou
- Lima Bean
- Lincoln
- Lindsey
- Linguine (Guine)
- Little
- Little Red Girl (Red-Dog, Red Devil Dog, RedBull, RED)
- Loki
- Lola
- Longshot
- Loretta
- Loretta Lynn
- Lou
- Loudmouth McGee
- Loulu
- Louie
- Louise Nap-a-Pooper (Lula)
- Lousiana (Weezi-anna, Weezie)
- Lu
- Lucifer (Lucy)
- Lucy
- Ludo
- Luke

- Lula
- Lula Belle
- Lulu (Ruby Roo, Sweet Potato)
- Luna
- Lunabelle
- Lurlene
- Lyla
- Maeve
- Mabel
- Macey
- Maddux
- Maebe Beatrix
- Maggie
- Maggie Mae (Maga Daga Beanstalk)
- Magic
- Magnolia
- Maizey
- Maizey Moo
- Malcolm
- Maple
- Marabelle
- Marlee
- Marvel
- Matey May

- Mathilda (TilTil, Tilly Sue, Tilda Bear, Tilda Mae, Tilly Beans, Big Mouth)
- Marshal Raylan Givens
- Mary
- Mary Jane
- Matt
- Maverick
- Mavis
- Max
- Maya
- Maya's Amazing Grace
- Maya's Jessa Grace
- Maybe
- Mazi
- Mazzy
- Mellifera
- Melvin
- Memphis
- Memphis Eugenie
- Memphis Louise
- Mercury Riverdog (Big Dog, Damnit)
- Mercy
- Mia
- Mika
- Mike

- Millie
- Milo
- Minnie Man
- Minnie Mouse
- Mirra
- Mirra Belle
- Miss Bluebell
- Miss Grace
- Miss Kitty
- Miss Maizee Jean
- Miss Molly
- Miss Pickles
- Miss Shy Violet Ann (Shy Vi)
- Miss Sweetpea
- Miss Taffy Lee
- Miss Trapper Tripod (Trap)
- Miss Tullamore Dew
- Missy
- Missy Barooo
- Mocha
- Mogley
- Molly
- Molly Sue
- Moose

- Moses
- Moss
- Moulson
- Mr. Beans
- Mr. Bojangles
- Mr. Buddy Bigglesworth
- Mr. Jack Daniels
- Muckley
- Mudd
- Murphy
- Murphy Brown
- Nash
- Navi
- Nellie
- Newton (Newt)
- Nexus
- Nina
- Nora
- Norman
- Nyla
- Nyx (goddess of night)
- Odin
- Ojibwe
- Ol' Dan Beau

- Oliver
- Oliver Queen (A.K.A. Sir Barksalot, Green Arrow)
- Ollie
- One-Eyed Si
- Opal
- Opal Long Legs
- Otis
- Otso
- Otter
- Otto
- Ovechkin
- Ovie
- Ozzie
- Paddy Cake
- Paisley
- Pancake
- Patch
- Patches
- Pattycake
- Peanut
- Pearl
- Penny
- Penny Lane
- Pepper Potts

- Petey
- Petunia
- Phebe
- Philly
- Phoenix
- Pi
- Picadilly Circus
- Pickles
- Piper
- Piper Marie
- Pixel
- Pizza
- Playboy
- Pocahontas
- Polly-Anne
- Poppy
- Porsche
- Possum
- Pretty Boy Pink Floyd
- Primo
- Prim Rose
- Princess Candy
- Quest
- Rabbit

- Radley
- Ragner (Rags, Raggy, Rag-O, Rag-a-Roni, Wildass)
- Rain
- Rainy
- Ranger
- Rastro (Astro with the speech impediment)
- Raylan
- Rebel
- Rebel Rouser
- Reese
- Reese Cup
- Reeses
- Reggie
- Remington
- Remy
- Renee
- Renner
- Rhapsody
- Rhett
- Rhianna
- Rhodie
- Ridge
- Ridonka-Tonks
- Riggins

- Riley
- Riley Rose
- River
- Roger
- Rollins Leadville
- Rooster
- Rorie
- Rory
- Rosa Lee
- Rosco
- Rosie
- Roxy
- Roy
- Roz
- Ruby
- Ruby Roo
- Ruby Roux
- Ruby Sue
- Ruckus
- Rufus
- Ruger
- Rusty
- Sadie
- Sage

- Sally
- Sammie
- Sasha
- Sassy
- Sauer
- Scarlet
- Scarlett
- Scout
- Screwie Louie
- Scurvy Dog
- Seamus
- Sebastian
- Sebastian Bach
- Shawn
- Shelby
- Shelby Rae
- Sherlock
- Shiloh
- Shooter
- Sideshot
- Skeet
- Skipper
- Sky Blue
- Slats Gilmore

- Sloan
- Sloane
- Slyder
- Smoke
- Smokey
- Smoky
- Snickers
- Snoopy
- Solo
- Sonny Dancer
- Sophie
- Sounder
- Spaghetti
- Special Ed
- Spock
- Spruce
- Squeaky
- Stan
- Stanley Michael
- Star
- Stella
- Stonewall Jackson (Jackson)
- Storm
- Stormy

- Strider
- Stryker
- Stuart
- Sugar
- Sully
- Summer
- Sunflower
- Sunshine
- Susie
- Sutton
- Suzy
- Swampy (Swamp Ass)
- Sweet Pea
- Sy
- Taffy
- Talla
- Tally
- Tap
- Tara
- Taters
- Teddy
- Tex
- Thea
- The Biscuit

- Tikka
- Timber
- Titan
- Toby
- Tommy
- Tom Sawyer (Thomas)
- Torrey
- Tremor
- Tress
- Trigger
- Trooper
- Tucker
- Tucker Jon
- Tuco
- Tullamore Dew
- Tululadew
- Tundra
- Turk
- Tusker
- Tyson Bartholomew
- Valentine
- Vega
- Venus
- Viktor

- Vladimir
- Waffles
- Waggle Baggins
- Walker
- Waltzing Matilda (Matilda, Tilly, Droolie, Ma-Kill-Da)
- Waylon
- Waylon Jennings (Way-Jay)
- Wednesday
- Weezie
- Weller
- Wendall
- Wesson
- Weston
- Whaylond
- Wherli
- Wilbur
- Wild Bob
- Wilkes
- Willow
- Wilma
- Wilson
- Winnie
- Woobit
- Woodrow

- Woodstock

- Woody

- Xerxes

- Yoda

- Yogi

- Yogi Bear

- Zcaro

- Zeke

- Zelda

- Zippy

- Zoey

- Zuc

Aside from their personal, proper, Christian names, our sweet and wonderful coonhounds have been referred to as *"goonhounds," "hell hounds," "conhounds," "drama hounds,"* and *"coonholes."*

I present to you Exhibit A.

We thought Beau and Lou were coonhounds. We were wrong. They are *con*hounds…

Lou: Now, you remember the plan, right? You tell Daddy that you have to go potty. I'll pretend I'm sleeping. After you come in, Daddy will give us each a nomnom.

Beau: Yeah. Then you tell Mommy that you have to go out. Then when you come in, she'll give us each another nomnom.

It works every time!

Both: Hehehehe! We're so smart!

"Hell hounds" has been used in several instances by several different people. The latest was in regard to the coonhounds barking incessantly and were so intimidating that trick-or-treaters wouldn't even come up to the door for candy. So Mom and Dad, while feeling bad for the kids, got the chocolate (a dozen bags) all to themselves!

And "coonholes?" Well, I'll just leave it at that. Sometimes dinner is swiped off the counter or things are torn up, and therefore the patience of moms and dads wears a bit thin, thereby causing said parents to utter said alias.

But we all know that all coonhounds are absolute angels, don't we? And people who rescue and love coonhounds are also angels. Here's proof:

When my husband and I adopted Roger three years ago, we thought something was up with him. He was a bit aloof, didn't show much affection, was only interested in sniffing around the house, etc. I didn't get it. I'd only had Labs. Why didn't he show affection right away? We'd never had a hound before; we had no clue what to expect.

Two days later we took our new coonhound rescue to a nearby arts and music festival to walk around. Bad idea. (Looking back, I understand this wasn't good for a new hound rescue, so please, no judgment.) Things turned from bad to worse as Roger was so stressed out from the loud festival music. We returned to the car confused and stressed.

When we got to our car, a woman approached us out of nowhere. She said, "Oh, you have a hound there don't you. Hounds are special. They're different."

I'll never forget those words. We call her our "Coonhound Angel" because she perfectly described the Coonhound. Special. And different.

One name that popped up and intrigued me was Scurvy Dog. Here are two separate posts about how he got his name:

...We rescued a walker hound last week that is very underweight. We named him Scurvy Dog because he has scars and the grandkids like pirates. He's so precious, gets along with our cats and other animals on the mountain. I got my first face lick yesterday...

We named him Scurvy because the hubby and grandsons are into pirates. He had battle scars when we adopted him and was so emaciated that it fit. He also responded to it best. You can no longer see his ribs or hips and he's learning to play.

Just as Casey is named after my great-grandfather, I'm sure much thought and many emotions have been involved in naming these special hounds, as well as some of the unique spelling of names. I became intrigued and eager to learn how people decided, and came up with, names for their coonhounds, so I sent out a request on LWMRC. My fellow coonhound lovers didn't disappoint and I got a bunch of responses! Many responses included heart, smiling and laughing emojis. Here are some responses, in no particular order. Some of the responses contained photographs, so I have edited the responses by deleting out references to the photos without changing the way in which the names were chosen. Enjoy!

[Ann Underwood Jayne] Best of luck on your book. It warms my heart to know even more people can be made aware of how wonderful these dogs are. About Floyd's name…I had a 3-hr. drive home with him and I kept asking him how my pretty boy was doing. So then I thought of the gangster. We listened to Tom Petty and Pink Floyd on the drive home. Since his previous owner had called him Ferd (no typo here!), I figured Floyd would be an easy transition for a name change. I had considered naming him after Tom Petty, but the day after Floyd joined us, Oct. 1, 2017, Tom Petty died the next day.

A photo of Floyd was on LWMRC. Floyd's owner added this: "Floyd in the cat bed in the bedroom. His full name? Pretty Boy Pink Floyd."

Introducing the B-Boys: Bedrich, Bastian, Barnaby, Bixby, Benedict, Bishop and Bronson. Bedrich is taken from the Czech composer Bedrich Smetana. Bishop was named after Robert Redford's character in *Sneakers* and also from an episode of *King of the Hill*.

I was a one-hound owner too but these special guys were an accidental litter that came tumbling into my life unexpectedly. It's a really unusual situation.

It was quite chaotic for the first two years, even those people who choose to adopt large packs tend to bring them in one at a time. That way you just have to train your first dog really well and he or she will model those good behaviors for the next dog and so forth. They always advise against adopting even a pair of puppy siblings together so by taking on the septpuplets, I've resigned myself to living in a friendly hound mosh pit.

They sort of know their names but not completely, mostly because I've never been a very disciplined person when it comes to diligent training. Now that they're three and calmer, I really need to devote one-on-one time to train them.

They each have crates that they sleep in at night and I give them each a Milk Bone every time they go into their crates so they quickly learned whose crate is whose and they eagerly go in them when it's meal time, nap time, or bed time.

For telling them apart, I assigned them each a different color when I first brought them home, and primarily use their collars to ID them at a glance, although they do have slightly different marking variations and personalities so it's possible to distinguish them without their collars if you're familiar with them.

Our dog was named after Candace, the lady who pulled her just two hours before she was to be killed. I added Princess to her name, hence Princess Candy.

We have named all of our dogs (and cats) after mountains in Colorado. We have had a Torrey, Kelso, Tucker and Avery.

We named Clementine because she's reddish/orange and she was so sweet when we first met her. She's a girly dog and it seemed like a girly name. But as the weeks went on, we discovered that she has a lot of sass, too. Thus, her nickname Lemon. We call her a *sour patch hound.*

Our Treeing Walker Coonhound is named Bleu Cheese. He got the name because the ticking on his coat reminded me of the salad dressing! I always tell him that I know it ain't easy being Cheesy! We have a little dog named Gigi, because that's the name she came with and it stuck.

I lost my hound, Lola, a week after surgery for ovarian cancer. I was devastated. I saw this beautiful hound that was being fostered in Virginia who was named Ann. I fell in love with her sweet face. So, I filled out an application and was approved. When talking to the foster mom, she kept saying that Ann was so shy. When I told my friend that she was shy, my friend said, "Oh! She is just a shy Violet!" I thought that was perfect! So, my dog's name is Miss Shy Violet Ann. Shy Vi!

Blue was #9 of a litter of 10 (even the label on his crate at the rescue had him as #9). My husband was a baseball umpire so it made perfectly logical sense to call him Blue!

My kid's name is Rooster. I got him from the town of Chester and he didn't have a name. All I could think of was Chester's Chicken! So he wound up being called Rooster!

Sadie was originally Lady, then renamed Haley at the shelter (there was already a Lady). Lady was my childhood dog's name. Haley is my daughter's name. I named her Sadie for the similar vowel sounds. And also after a long-dead Southern great-aunt. We think it suits her.

Waggle Baggins was brought to Denver on a transport van from Ardmore, Oklahoma as a puppy. We wanted a puppy and a friend for our beagle, Sweet Pea. We immediately fell in love with her face and I stalked the Dumb Friends League website for days until she was available for adoption. We picked her up before getting our youngest child from school. She wiggled and waggled so excitedly when she met him! Then, once home, our older two kids came in one at a time from the busses and she waggled her whole body. She was so excited to have so many kids! The Waggles part is pretty obvious (also my Grandfather had a beagle named Wiggles when he was a kid so I liked the nostalgic part). As she grew, her feet became massive (and she was such a KLUTZ) and furry, so I started teasing that she was a Hobbitt. This is how she was given a last name! Waggle Baggins! It's fun to say, too!

My last hound was named Copper. I always loved that name. My dog now is named Floyd but as a nickname we call him Moochy Von Moochenstein because he's always mooching off Barry McBarksalot, who loves to bark and howl.

FedEx, my loving beagle, was found by the FedEx lady. My husband and I had Sophie, our black and tan coonhound (our first child) and the night before FedEx came into our lives, we had decided that Sophie needed a sibling but it could only be a hound. She is the reason we will always rescue and have a special spot in our hearts for ALL hounds. Anyway, I went to work with him the next day (he owned an auto repair shop) and our local FedEx lady came in delivering a car part and told us about a puppy she saw a week ago in the neighborhood. She saw it and thought the owners would be looking for it as a tropical storm was about to hit over the weekend. She saw him a week later wandering in the streets, with no tag, unneutered and eating out of a trash can. She picked him up after coming to us and telling us about him. Right then my husband and I said we would take him to the vet and have him scanned for a chip. No chip. She took him around all day doing her local deliveries, asking people about his potential owners. No one gave her any leads. At the end of her shift she brought him to us. We tried to do the right thing and looked for his owners for months. Six months later we got him fixed and chipped and officially named him after a great company and lady. Later on she was recognized by FedEx as a model employee for doing the right thing in the community. Both she and FedEx our beagle were featured in the FedEx internal newsletter!

Kolsch is the third in a series of beer-themed dogs. The first was a Labrador retriever named Barley because she was born behind the Barley Mill Pub in Portland. The second was a six-week-old male puppy. Tap was black and fluffy and built for snow. Tap, as in beer tap, and appropriate for a boy. Kolsch fit the criteria for the color of the dog and also something that could be easily yelled and not everyone will know what it means.

Our Layla had four names and homes before coming to us. She is lovely and loved, also kind of a challenge. I think that's what Eric Clapton thought about his Layla, too. She came to that name right away.

My husband did not want another dog. He was born in Valdosta, Georgia so I chose Georgia On My Mind to endear him to her. It worked.

We always keep the names that the rescue gave them. The poor dog has enough adjusting to do. We don't want to confuse them more.

Sounder made sense since she was brought from a deplorable situation in California up to Seattle in the Puget Sound.

I have Bumpus, a blue tick and Rooster, a Redbone! Bumpus is from the movie *A Christmas Story* (the Bumpus hounds). We got Rooster from *The Ranch*.

My husband is very knowledgeable about the Civil War and likes "there he stood like a stone wall." So, we have Stonewall Jackson, Jackson for short.

My Magnolia was turned in to the Gulfport, Mississippi Humane Society at eight-months old. She was sent to the Cleveland, Ohio APL where I adopted her. I named her Magnolia because that's Mississippi's state flower. She is now 13-1/2 years old.

I have gone back in the family tree to pick names.

Pickles is our son's dog who is now pretty much mine. We call our son Dyl a lot so Pickles became his dog's name. It fits her perfectly and it is hard not to smile when you say it. It's hard not to smile when you look at her adorable goofiness.

I named my first black and tan Maya because I was on my way home from seeing an exhibit of Mayan artifacts when I found her. I named the next one Maya's Amazing Grace and the third one Maya's Jessa Grace because I felt I should honor Maya for bringing me so much love. My first bluetick was named Billy Jack because he was a big, gentle rebel and his successor is Billy Jack's One Tin Soldier. My first Treeing Walker Coonhound was Sonny Dancer because he always danced instead of walking. My current TWC/Plott Hound is Angel Dancer. I had another name in mind for Angel but every time I called her that, she would look at me in disgust and walk away. One day I said what an angel she is and she danced around me and wagged her tail, so she became Angel Dancer.

∝✕⊃

I call my boy Houndy McHounderson. Lol.

∝✕⊃

Newt, officially Newton, is named after his rescuer's hometown of Newton, TN.

∝✕⊃

Lilo was my hound's name when we got her and this was one of the reasons I called about her. One of my favorite movies is *Lilo and Stitch*. When she gets into trouble, I call her Experiment 626.

∝✕⊃

Dempsey came with that name. I've wanted to change it for the past eight years but my husband said no. LOL. All rescues give the dogs new names as they come in so it would have been so easy to change his name. We were the ones who reinforced that name.

∝✕⊃

I got a hound that was found on the side of the road, bug-eaten, losing hair, emaciated and had a broken pelvis. His one leg just hung there, without being able to put weight on it. I fostered him and helped nurse him back to health. He walked with a stiff leg at first. We thought he looked like Chester on *Gunsmoke*. But we already had a Chester, so he got named Dillon, like the marshal. Oh, he's ours now. Sweetest dog ever!

We adopted Daisy as an adult, so we kept her name. The rescue called her Daisy Mae and my niece's middle name is Mae, so we changed it to Lou, as in Lou Reed. Every dog that I've had in my adult life so far has been named after a musician. Sebastian Bach (as in Skid Row), Bruce Springsteen (self-explanatory), and now Daisy Lou!

Ike was surrendered with his litter mate. They were Mike and Ike (yes, like the candy, lol). After bringing him home I decided to give him a formal name (for when he is in trouble or just simply not listening) and settled on Icarius. In Greek mythology, Icarius was a Roman king who was a fast runner and wouldn't allow his daughter to marry unless her suitor could beat him in a race. He was beaten by Odysseus who is the main character in *The Odyssey*. My Ike is pretty quick for a hound and genuinely believes he is royalty, so I found it fitting.

Cera was originally Sally S'more and she's so NOT the fru-fru dog that name sort of lends itself to. The name "Cera" came from the movie *The Land Before Time* (the character was a triceratops) who is a rough-and-tumble bossy pants and boy does she fit that mold! We get asked all the time if we named her after Michael Cera. LOL.

Huckleberry's original name was Ben but he had ZERO recall/recognition of it. We were fostering him and watching the movie *Tombstone* when the line, "I'm your Huckleberry" struck a chord with us and that was that. Plus he's such a doof and I love that the name just fits him perfectly!

Kaboom was in a very bleak situation in Montana. Just another high-kill shelter in rural America. He was scheduled to die around the 4th of July. He did not go Kaboom because he was saved and was quickly adopted and renamed Fenway. A wonderful 16-year-old young man adopted him and gave that dog the best life on the planet. The adopter was from Boston originally and had a soft spot in his heart for Fenway Park, so it all made sense.

Our Magnolia came from the pound with the name Waggin', I assume because of the tail, which is, indeed, constantly wagging. We deemed her Magnolia because her breed is more common in the south (she's a red tick) and I lived in Magnolia, Texas for a few years. We call her all sorts of things, such as Waffle, Waffley, Houndy, etc. She's ridiculous and we love her so much.

Finn's name was originally Kenny, but the rescue had it written weird on his tag and it looked like Finne. All of our dogs have had a fishing-themed name. There was Fly and Fisher. When we lost Fisher, we adopted Reel and when we lost Fly, we adopted Finn. Finn was in a fenced-off area at the rescue with his siblings and he was covered in poop, only because one of the puppies pooped and apparently all of the puppies walked through it and over each other, not because the rescue was bad. He insisted I pick him up instead of one of his non-poop siblings. I fell in love right then. When we saw his name and thought it said Finn, we thought it was meant to be! Best decision ever!

My little girl came from West Virginia. She was found on top of a mountain with a trap on her back leg. So I failed at fostering her. We named her Miss Trapper Tripod!

Lulu is named after Boss Hogg's wife from *The Dukes of Hazzard*. We also have several nicknames for her, including Sweet Potato and Ruby Roo.

My hubby wouldn't agree to name our baby girl Penny, so the pup got the name.

Elvis is aptly named because he's nothing but a hound dog. He came from the shelter with that name and we kept it.

One-Eyed Si is what the rescue called our hound, and we kept the name.

I'm usually the "namer" in the family, but since my hubby found Buddy, I said, "You name him." Whilst trying to think of a name, he was calling him Buddy. You can see how far his imagination went.

When I adopted my boy, he came to us with the name Joey. I really wanted something special and unique, not an everyday dog name. As we started tossing around potential names, the name Renner really spoke to me. It is my mom's maiden name so the family connection was really special. For me, it's a way of honoring that side of my family tree.

A couple of months before my father died, we rescued our bluetick who came to us with the name Aurora. My father said that is too much to say! So, we changed it to Rorie and he was right. Our red tick was called Bonnie, but it didn't feel right. Our friend helped me find a name that reflected her breed...she became Ruby.

Ruby Roux was named Bobo at the shelter (totally unfitting for a beautiful red-headed beauty like her). My little brother adopted her and named her Ribley. After a couple of months with him in college, she kept becoming a flight risk and his living on a major interstate became a worry. He asked us to take her in to find her a new home shortly after my baby of nine years, Keyli, succumbed to doggie diabetes. In the first hours of being in our home, she walked with my son (who is borderline autistic) straight to his room and when I followed behind a couple of moments later, she was laying in the floor and had train tracks connected across her back like a giant coonhound suspension bridge. My husband immediately said, "Well, she's not going anywhere." We had to change her name because my kids could NOT say Ribley despite our best efforts. Later my kids came to us saying we should call her Ru because that's how she howled. And thus Ruby (for her redbone coat) Roux came to be.

I wanted to name Blue Remy after Dennis Quaid's character in *The Big Easy*, but I have a colleague named Renie. And even before I actually got the pup, I accidentally called Renie Remy. I knew that would never fly, LOL. I also thought it would be fun to name a bluetick "Blue" so that was Plan B. Little did I know that half the blueticks out there are named Blue. Also his foster mom had already started calling him Blue, so it was a sign. And he does love to sing the blues. Arroooo!

My first hound was Sassy, named for jazz singer Sarah Vaughan. Sassy did love to sing, and she lived up to her name— full of sass. (She has a sister named Ella, for Ella Fitzgerald.) I always swore that I was going to name my next dog Serena, lol.

I was only half-heartedly looking for another dog. I was waiting for a sign that the right dog had come along and to be honest, my setter would be a hard one to beat because she truly was that perfect. Enter Facebook. The Midwest Animal Rescue posted Susie's picture that she was ready for adoption and the world stopped. I fell head over heels. I drove out and took her home that night. Her shelter name was Susie, and I decided to keep it because my great-grandmother's childhood nickname was Susie. Her name was Stella and I know it makes zero sense and no one remembers how she got that nickname. Anyway, my great-grandmother was a HUGE animal lover and I know I got that from her. I decided to keep her name in honor of my Nenaw, because I think her name was my sign. Without any doubt she would love Susie, and she is the only person I know who wouldn't mind having a dog named after her.

✦

Finn (formerly known as Buddy) was named after Huckleberry Finn because where I got him was in the country.

✦

We are really original and my five-year-old named our dog Copper after *The Fox and the Hound* and also because of his coat color. His name at the rescue was Reese and I liked that but the five-year-old vetoed it.

✦

I named my dog Chase, after Chase Eliot, my favorite NASCAR driver. My wife thinks it is because he likes to chase things.

Riggins came from a local rescue here in Raleigh. His original name at the Wake County Animal Shelter was Timothy. The rescue were big fans of *Friday Night Lights* so Timothy became Riggins after the character Tim Riggins. He was found locked in an abandoned trailer, starved down to 30 pounds. Seven years later he is doing great and getting to a ripe old senior of 14 years.

Max, aka Maximus you are a pain in our Aximus. God bless his heart. He passed away on Saturday (April 2020) at age 15…loved forever.

Our current Redbone came to us named Chloe, but never answered to it. We changed her name to Lousiana, but our three-year-old granddaughter pronounces it Weezi-anna. So the Coonhound is now called Weezie.

Our Winnie is named after the character Winnie Cooper from the TV show *The Wonder Years*.

Suffice it to say, rescued coonhounds deserve, and get, special names. Even if their rescuing angel can't think of an exotic name, the names they choose are special, making these coonhounds their very own. Making them special. Bringing them into something of which they've never been a part. They make them family.

Chapter 12

Hunting Dog Exception

Someone in LWMRC made a disturbing post that alerted coonhound lovers to an exemption in South Carolina's laws regarding abandonment of animals. I was appalled and disgusted. It was sickening. It resonated with me and is one of the reasons I wrote this book. Until Casey and I rescued each other, I was ignorant of the plight of so many coonhounds in the United States.

But after reading about this law on Facebook, and then looking it up for myself (still effective as of 2017), I decided that animal cruelty laws needed to be incorporated into this book.

The South Carolina law regarding abandonment of animals, including dogs, states:

> § 47-1-70. Abandonment of animals; penalties; hunting
> dog exception

A. A person may not abandon an animal. As used in this section "abandonment" is defined as deserting, forsaking, or intending to give up absolutely an animal without securing another owner or without providing the necessities of life. "Necessities of life" includes:

1. Adequate water which means a constant access to a supply of clean, fresh, and potable water provided in a suitable manner for the species;

2. Adequate food which means provision at suitable intervals of quantities of wholesome foodstuff suitable for the species and age, sufficient to maintain a reasonable level of nutrition to allow for proper growth and weight;

3. Adequate shelter which means shelter that reasonably may be expected to protect the animal from physical suffering or impairment of health due to exposure to the elements or adverse weather.

B. A person who violates this section is guilty of a misdemeanor and, upon conviction, must be fined not less than two hundred nor more than five hundred dollars or imprisoned not more than thirty days, or both. Offenses under this section must be tried in the magistrate's or municipal court.

C. A hunting dog that is positively identifiable in accordance with Section 47-3-510 or Section 47-3-530 is exempt from this section.

Did you catch that? Hunting dogs are *exempt* from abandonment and necessities of life regulations.

I looked up the other sections to see what identified a hunting dog. These sections are found in the 2017 South Carolina Code of Laws, Title 47 – Animals, Livestock and Poultry, Chapter 3 – Dogs and other Domestic Pets.

Section 47-3-510. Owner may register dog; fee.

The owner of any dog or kennel, may upon payment of a fee to be determined by the South Carolina Department of Natural Resources (department), not to exceed five dollars a dog or twenty dollars a kennel, have his dog registered by the department and the registration number tattooed in either of the dog's ears or on any other clearly visible part of the body that would be considered most suitable for the respective species of dog. The department shall maintain records of the names and addresses of the owners of registered kennels.

Section 47-3-530. Penalties for stealing or killing identifiable dog.

Any person stealing any positively identifiable dog is guilty of a misdemeanor and upon conviction must be fined not less than five hundred dollars nor more than one thousand dollars or imprisoned for not less than thirty days nor more than six months, or both.

Any person killing any dog when owner may be identified by means of a collar bearing sufficient information or some other form of positive identification is guilty of a misdemeanor and upon conviction must be fined not less than five hundred dollars nor more than one thousand dollars or imprisoned for not less than thirty days nor more than six months, or both. This paragraph does not apply to the killing of a dog threatening to cause or causing personal injury or property damage.

I'm not a lawyer. But my amateur understanding of this law is that anyone who owns any type of hunting dog can pay a fee, register the dog, get it tattooed, and then abandon it without any repercussions. Not only are coonhounds and foxhounds included, but so are beagles, Basset hounds, dachshunds, Weimaraners, Labrador retrievers, golden retrievers, German short-haired pointers, spaniels, setters, etc. *Hunting dogs.*

In South Carolina, if an "owner," and I use that term loosely, has several black and tan coonhounds and decides he no longer wants them—no longer wants to feed them, wants younger ones, maybe they're gun shy, he decides he wants blueticks, whatever—he can simply dump, throw away, discard, *abandon* the dogs. And guess what? There are *zero* repercussions for him. He (or she) is protected by the South Carolina law. The poor dogs aren't. But the humans are free to do this again. And again. And again. This is heart-breaking. And infuriating. And asinine. And cruel.

My research into the South Carolina law piqued my interest. What about Oklahoma? What about other southern states where coonhounds are prevalent? What about all 50 states? Are there any other states who allow hunting dogs to be abandoned, to be denied basic necessities like food, water, and proper shelter?

I discovered a Michigan State University website that contains every law regarding animals in each of the 50 states. If you want to check your state's laws, I highly recommend this site. Go to http://www.animallaw.info/statute and enter the state in which you are interested. I also printed off a summary of each state's animal cruelty laws from www.StrayPetAdvocacy.org. Illinois is listed as **Model Law** for this website. This gives the website for each state's legislation on animal cruelty. It did not, however, list the hunting dog exemption in South Carolina's laws. I went back to the Michigan State University web site and skimmed through each state's laws.

Whew.

My eyes were opened. My focus was on cruelty and abandonment. However, other categories popped up that I really hadn't thought about. I'll get to them later. I momentarily considered applying to law school to become an advocate for abused animals.

First of all, I want to say that aside from South Carolina, the other 49 states do not have an exemption for abandoning hunting dogs. That's the good news.

Ohio does allow cruelty exemptions for dogs used in hunting or field trial purposes. Specifically, it is mentioned in Ohio Revised Code Annotated. Title IX. Agriculture-Animals-Fences. Chapter 959. Offenses Relating to Domestic Animals.

§959.131Cruelty Against Companion Animal defines cruelty in §959.131(A). The prohibitions of committing cruel acts against companion animals, that also pertains to owners, managers and employees of dog kennels are listed in §959.131(B), (C), (D), (E), and (F).

§959.131(G) Divisions (B), (C), (D), (E) and (F) of this section do not apply to any of the following:

1. A companion animal used in scientific research conducted by an institution in accordance with the federal animal welfare act and related regulations;

...

3. Dogs being used or intended for use for hunting or field trial purposes, provided that the dogs are being treated in accordance with usual and commonly accepted practices for the care of hunting dogs;

Note that I didn't list (2), (4), and (5). They deal with veterinarians, training devices and administering medicine, the latter of which is under Chapter 4741 of the Revised Code.

What troubles me about this exception is what I have learned about coonhound "training" and "treatment" ever since Casey came into my life.

As I said, Casey was skin and bones with a raw spot on his neck, presumably from being chained or tied up. The spot is still there, the hair forever rubbed away to the follicle.

ARLO was made aware of a Treeing Walker Coonhound and a Black and Tan Coonhound confined to a pen without food and water. The grass and weeds had grown up around the pens, which were not too far from a house.

Steve, one of ARLO's volunteers, went out to feed the dogs and get them some water. Of course, the dogs gobbled up the food. And now they actually had fresh water without mosquito larvae in it. Heartworms, anyone? Surprisingly, they had a covering over part of their pen so they could at least have a little shade. There were also chewed up plastic barrels for beds.

The sheriff got involved, as the owner didn't want anyone trespassing to feed his dogs. He wanted them hungry so they would hunt better. So, ARLO was no longer permitted to check on the dogs. The sheriff did say he would check on the dogs and make sure they're getting fed, albeit sporadically.

So that's part of coonhound training. Keep the dogs hungry. How much energy do they have when they haven't eaten for a couple of days? What about dehydration? Did the owner skip any meals? Was he hungry when he hunted? I doubt it. I'm guessing his belly was full.

I pray every night for those dogs and other dogs in similar situations. I pray for animals we don't know about; animals who are starving, confined, abandoned, abused. And I pray they are rescued.

Are other hunting dogs "trained" this way? I doubt if retrievers and pointers are. I sure hope not.

Each state outlines and defines abandonment, cruelty, aggravated cruelty, torture, and tormenting. They also define what necessities of life, shelter, confinement, and other things, including the type of animal, are. Without going into too much detail, cruelty and torture include intentionally knowing, maliciously or recklessly overloading, overdriving, tormenting, depriving of necessary sustenance or shelter, unnecessarily mutilating, maiming, poisoning, inflicting extreme physical pain (and prolonging the pain), starving, beating, physical suffering, injury, wounding or killing an animal in a cruel or inhumane manner.

The laws get specific regarding horses and donkeys, docking horses' tails, horse tripping, transporting animals, confinement (such as calves used for veal, so just don't eat veal, please), violations against service animals including police/military animals, dyeing animals such as chicks, ducks, and rabbits, and selling injured/crippled/sick animals. Additionally, dog tail docking, dew claw removal, ear cropping, devocalization, and Caesarian sections can only be performed by licensed veterinarians. So, this law is in place because people have once again found ways to be cruel by home-made operations.

There are 22 states, and Washington, D.C., which have anti-tethering laws. Hopefully this will expand to all 50 states soon. These states delineate the number of hours the dog can be tethered in a 24-hour period, specify the type of tether (and have outlawed some, such as choke collars, pinch collars, and prong type collars), the length and weight of the tether, require that the dog is allowed unencumbered access to food, water and shelter without becoming entangled, or tethering in certain weather conditions, such as extreme heat or cold, natural disasters (hurricanes, tropical storms, and tornado warnings).

States that do not have anti-tether laws can still penalize tethering a dog according to anti-cruelty laws if the dog suffers neglect or cruelty. Cities, towns and counties can enact and enforce their own anti-tethering laws.

Some states have laws which prohibit leaving animals in hot cars, too. Sadly, Oklahoma does not have an anti-tether law nor does it have a law prohibiting leaving animals in hot cars. Maybe I've found my next mission...

All states have various fines associated with cruelty to animals. Fines can range from $100 to $25,000. Some states return half of the money recovered in fines to animal rescue groups who turned in the violators. The charges range from misdemeanors to different classes of felonies, which can also include jail/prison time and prohibiting the felons from owning animals again. Oklahoma and other states have laws that may require the violator to pay for the cost of care, veterinary services, and boarding of the animals they victimized. Some states have provisions for the violators to undergo examinations and treatment from a psychiatrist.

Maine has an Animal Welfare Advisory Council. Maryland has an Animal Abuse Emergency Compensation Fund. Other states have officers specifically for investigating complaints, recovering the animals, and testifying at trials.

Good.

There are exceptions (it varies from state to state) for various categories:

- animal husbandry
- draft or pack animals
- equestrian teams
- exhibitions
- falconry
- farming
- herding of domestic animals
- horse racing
- hunting (not hunting dogs)

- live bait in fishing

- livestock shows

- operation of a zoological park or aquarium

- pest and rodent control

- pet shops

- processing for food or other commercial product

- religion

- research (scientific and medical)

- rodeos

- training

- trapping

- veterinary care

Not all states have all of these exemptions. Many of the states have several of them. And kudos to Minnesota which has "no named exemptions."

I realize there needs to be some exemptions or else certain groups or individuals could file claims against someone who is legitimately raising animals and caring for them. I'm just going to come right out and say it. There are groups that I think are terrorists. People for the Ethical Treatment of Animals (PETA) comes to mind, as does the Animal Liberation Front (ALF). While these groups claim to care about animals, what they really do is set fire to homes and businesses, turn animals loose, such as cattle and show horses, not to mention minks and other animals raised for fur.

Whether you wear fur or not, turning this many animals loose on the environment does not do the animals much good. These animals have been raised in captivity and are fed by humans every day. They don't have to look for their food. Now that they are loose, having this many predators loose will upset the balance of nature. They may eat more mice thereby taking away food from a wild animal. They may also become a meal for coyotes and hawks, which could cause their populations to increase, keeping more predators in the cycle, which means more competition for food.

PETA has a goal from their founder, Ingrid Newkirk, which is to outlaw anyone from owning an animal, be it a pet or livestock. Additionally, according to PETA, no one should be able to eat meat, wear leather or fur, or own/consume an animal in any way.

I can see where exceptions to rules come in. However, shouldn't certain training methods be brought into question? If someone sees a horse trainer beating a horse half to death because it wouldn't perform, is it really fair to the horse in that state that horse training is exempted from cruel treatment? Soring of the feet of Tennessee Walking Horses comes to mind. It's a perfectly accepted practice (for some), and unfortunately, it is protected by law.

On the other hand, what if a horse is acting up, not listening? The trainer gives it a smack with a riding crop. That's not cruel, but someone could perceive it as such and report them. I see why there are exceptions, I just think they should be more specific.

The Preventing Animal Cruelty and Torture (PACT) Act, was passed unanimously by the House of Representatives in October of 2019. The Senate passed it unanimously, as well on November 5, 2019. On November 25, 2019, President Donald J. Trump signed a bipartisan bill to make animal cruelty a federal felony, with up to seven years in prison!

PACT expands a 2010 law signed by former President Barack Obama that banned videos of animals being crushed, burned, drowned, suffocated, impaled, or suffering other forms of torture. It will help prosecutors address cases of abused animals that cross state lines and could also send more resources to investigate and prosecute animal cruelty cases.

While I certainly don't believe in government overreach, and although each state has its own anti-cruelty regulations, perhaps *now* charges of animal cruelty will be enforced via the state and/or federal government.

Research is another cloudy exception, in my opinion. I'm not talking about dogs and cats at the Purina facilities who get to sample new types of food or dogs who get baths to try out new shampoos. I'm referring to animals used to test for drugs and household hygiene and cleaning products

Animals used for medical testing to develop new drugs may be subject to discomfort. Perhaps the animal is intentionally infected with a disease in order to help find a cure. Hopefully there is no suffering and the animal is comfortable and/or humanely euthanized if it suffers too much.

What about animals, particularly beagles, raised specifically for research and experimentation? I've read too many stories about these poor dogs. Their lives are spent in cages, resulting in literally going stir crazy from constant confinement, and the only time they are released from the cages is to have masks put on them and toxic fumes pumped in the mask to see what effects it has on them. Isn't our society advanced enough to realize what poisons and toxins do? There is no need to subject these poor dogs, or any creature, to the effects of poison. And as posted on LWMRC, there is a company in one of the northern states seeking permission to build a research facility and breed/use coonhounds for testing.

What is wrong with people? Who gets up every day knowing they are going to hold a beagle while it squirms and tries to breathe and get away as someone else pours, squirts, or sprays toxic chemicals in their noses or down their throats? That's just wrong. Pray for these dogs, too.

Remember my story in Chapter 2 about Festus and other neighborhood dogs who disappeared? How we believed they were caught and taken to research facilities? It breaks my heart to think that Festus was probably subjected to some form of torture. And that it continues for other dogs. Other pets.

The state of Virginia has outlawed research facilities from using pets as research subjects. Their law, §3.2-6547 Acceptance of animals for research or experimentation; prohibition, states:

> No person shall use or accept for the purpose of medical research or experimentation any animal bearing a tag, license, or tattooed identification, unless the individual who owns such animal consents thereto in writing.

Tags can be removed. Licenses can be lost. And, in my opinion, any owner who consents to having his/her pet submitted to a research facility needs to be stuck in that cage next to, or instead of, their pet.

§4:22-59 of the New Jersey cruelty statutes provides restrictions upon the use of traditional animal testing if an appropriate alternative testing method is available. However, it also delineates that the federal government may allow animal testing if they determine that the non-animal alternative test does not assure the health of safety of consumers.

In February 2020, some U.S. states began considering banning the sale and importation of cosmetics that have been tested on animals! California, Nevada, and Illinois have already passed laws that take effect in 2020 banning the sales and importations of cosmetics tested on animals. Hawaii, Maryland, New Jersey, New York, and Virginia have been introducing similar bills since 2014.

Many cosmetic companies have already stopped animal testing. This practice is already banned in Europe and India. China, however, is very much opposed to this idea as they *require* animal testing for cosmetics (makeup, perfume, hair care products). "Special use" products produced in China, such as hair dye, sunscreen and whitening products, also require animal testing.

So, the bills passed in California, Nevada, and Illinois exempt any cosmetics sold in China and will allow those products to be tested on animals since Chinese law requires that. I'm thinking that that is just too bad. If Americans are using these products and aren't dropping dead, chances are Chinese people who use these products are not destined for death either. It's a good start, but animal testing on cosmetics and household cleaners needs to come to a screeching halt.

Reviewing the laws of each state led to some pleasant surprises, too. All 50 states have banned dog fighting. Some states elaborated on animal fighting to include outlawing baiting animals. Other animals, besides dogs, and activities that were listed and prohibited include: bears, bulls, cocks, hogs, other creatures, bull baiting, bear wrestling. Additionally, fighting paraphernalia is banned. The following are summarized from Nebraska's state laws, §28-1005.01(2)(a)(i-viii):

- breaking sticks - inserted behind the molars of the dog to break its grip on whatever animal or object it has in its jaws

- cat mill – a device that rotates around a central support, one arm secures the dog and one arm secures a cat, rabbit or other small animal just beyond the reach/grasp of the dog

- treadmill

- fighting pit – a walled area that provides a place for the animals to fight

- spring pole – a biting surface attached to a stretchable device that is suspended at a height that prevents the dog from reaching the biting surface while touching the ground

- heel – any edged or pointed instruments attached to the leg of a fowl

- boxing glove/muff – a protective device that covers the spurs of a fowl
- any other instrument commonly used in the furtherance of pitting an animal against another.

Who thinks of these things? I mean, someone has to really sit down and think about ways to torture an animal for fighting or to be used as bait. (I found out later that there is another way people thought of to harm these poor bait dogs. Keep reading.) If people want to box and beat the crap out of each other, go right ahead. Enjoy that brain damage later in life. But don't subject animals to your cruelty and stupidity. Maybe we should put these people in a cat mill next to a bear or lion or pit bull and see how that works out for them. I'm guessing it wouldn't be terribly fun or entertaining.

I purchased a copy of *The Lost Dogs* by Jim Gorant. It is about the dogs seized from Michael Vick, the NFL player who was arrested for dog fighting. I'm steeling myself to read this book. Suzy, a friend, fellow dog rescuer, and yogi, read it and said she had to put it down and take walks. I think I might have to wait to read this book because of a dog I met, sweet Ruby, in August 2020.

Valerie and Brett are restoring Brett's grandfather's old dairy barn. Brett was mowing the pasture and two stray dogs ran up to him. They were skin and bones and covered in ticks. He called Valerie to bring out some dog food. When she arrived, two more dogs had shown up. One of them, the one who was in the worst shape, was a pit bull. It was obvious that she had had a litter of puppies; probably several litters. The other three dogs were mixed breed dogs. Two of them were pups, probably less than a year old. All four were starving and devoured the dog food Brett and Valerie gave them.

After the dogs had eaten, they rested in the shade of the wooden stairs going to the top story of the barn. They had full tummies, water, and were safe. Andrea's husband, Jeff, dipped them for ticks, except one who was shy and wouldn't come up to anyone.

That night, our mother, who is in the nursing home in Okemah, suffered a stroke, so I came to Okemah the next day. A storm also blew in later that night, and the dogs left. Valerie had called ARLO, and they were sending someone out to get the dogs and take them to a foster home the next day. But now the dogs were nowhere to be found. It was heartbreaking, and I prayed they would come back.

Since we thought it was the end for Mama, while I worried about the dogs, I was more concerned for her. This was also *still* during Covid-19 so we had not been able to get near Mama as the nursing home was on lockdown. This was probably going to be the last time we would see Mama so the director allowed us in to see Mama. We had to wear the protective clothing, masks, and gloves, but at least I could touch my mother one more time and give her a kiss.

I came back to Okemah the next day, Friday. Mama was a little better. I came back on Saturday with Jennifer and her daughter, Rachel. The dogs had returned. While Jennifer and Rachel visited Mama, I went with Valerie and Cale to see the dogs and wait for ARLO to come get them.

Camden and Cale had named the dogs. Ruby was the pit bull mama. The other dogs were Lily, probably a pit-bull mix, and two smaller pups that looked like beagle/sheltie mix. They were named Boomer and Sooner. Boomer was the shy pup, and he still wouldn't come up to us. Sooner stayed close to Ruby, so I don't know if they were her pups or not. They really didn't look like they were pit bulls. I'm guessing they were just unfortunate pups that had been advertised as "free dogs" and ended up in hell.

Ruby wagged her tail when I walked up. As I sat down to pet her, she sidled up next to me and began licking my cheek, being very affectionate. Her sweet face was scarred up. She was missing part of a toe. Her ears were chewed up. When I looked in her mouth to see approximately how old she was, I almost became sick to my stomach. Ruby's teeth had been filed down to the gums. Someone had thought of another cruel thing to do to dogs. If your teeth are filed down, there's no way to fight back and defend yourself from the fighting dog that is attacking you. Add another bullet to the list of things people think of to torture dogs.

It was clear that these four dogs had been used as bait dogs and Ruby had also been used for breeding. She had been completely used up in every way possible, and now she had been thrown away. Discarded. Oh, she and Lily and Sooner had on collars. But they weren't pets. Or loved. Their legs were chewed up as well, and Sooner had lots of scratches and bite marks on her young belly.

Cale asked me why they always find stray dogs. (To date they have taken in/rescued/adopted 13 dogs.) I told him, as I started to cry, that God sends these dogs to us because He knows that we will take care of them.

Valerie got more food out but the dogs weren't terribly hungry. Ruby and Sooner dozed in the shade beneath the stairs. Poor Ruby had been so hungry that she had been able to eat the hard kibble. I guess she can still crunch with the remnants of her molars. Boomer and Lily got under the truck. I sat down next to Ruby and Sooner and stroked Ruby. She sighed and thumped her tail. Cale played with Sooner with a long blade of grass.

For all that these dogs had been through, there wasn't a mean or aggressive bone in their bodies. They had been totally abused and failed by humans and had every right to hate and not trust. But they didn't. They had love to give. They knew that now they were safe.

I was 99% sure I was taking Ruby home. I knew that there was also a 99% chance that I would end up in divorce court. About that time, Jaime, the ARLO president, and her husband, Tony, showed up to get the dogs.

We had a little trouble getting Boomer. He would run away from us, but he wouldn't run far away. Finally he went under the truck. Jaime spoke kindly to him while I was able to hold his hind legs and Tony could put a slip leash around Boomer's neck. Jaime scooped Boomer up in her arms, and he melted. He didn't try to bite. He didn't try to get away. He was as gentle as a lamb.

So now these dogs will be fed and loved and vetted and spayed/neutered. Boomer, Sooner and Lily have already been accepted to an out-of-state rescue, so they will have brand new homes and lives. No more cruelty for them. Ruby had to get fattened up, but she was quickly adopted into a loving home! God is at work. And I didn't get divorced.

On Sunday, Mama was able to sit up and talk a little. She knew us and once again, we could touch her and kiss her. She asked me if I had a good life. I told her I had a very good life and that she and Daddy had given me a good life. She smiled and said, "We did have a good life." Yes, we did.

While I was doing my research, there was one other subject I hadn't even considered until I skimmed through all 50 of the state laws. Bestiality. I'm not even touching that one. It's hard to wrap my head around the ways people can be cruel to an animal. And just when I thought the states had exhausted practically everything, they saved this one for last.

Read your state's laws. If there is something missing, contact your state representatives. Cite other state laws on the subject that are missing in your state. Check with local rescue groups about statistics.

Start with your own town. Since Okemah, Oklahoma, enacted spay/neuter laws, maybe they'll enact anti-tethering laws. Maybe other cities and towns will incorporate spaying and neutering into their laws. This can only grow and maybe eventually, it will expand into a state law.

It's so disheartening and sickening to read about ways people think of to be cruel. But at least some people are waking up! Isn't it a glorious thought to think that we could get to the point in time where animal cruelty is outlawed and enforced so that it doesn't exist? And that pet overpopulation stops, and animal shelters and rescue organizations have empty kennels because there aren't any strays or unwanted dogs. That would truly be a "Hallelujah!" day!

Chapter 13

Stories of Coonhound Rescues

Love is patient, love is kind and is not jealous; love does not brag and is not arrogant, does not act unbecomingly; it does not seek its own, is not provoked, does not take into account a wrong suffered, does not rejoice in unrighteousness, but rejoices with the truth, bears all things, hopes all things, endures all things.
LOVE NEVER FAILS.

1 Corinthians 13:4-8

C asey opened my eyes to the plight of coonhounds all across the United States. Little did I know how many of these sweet souls were being starved, beaten, shot, abandoned, dumped, left tied up, abused and neglected. No animal or human should ever be subject to this kind of treatment.

After reading some stories of how people acquired their coonhounds in LWMRC, I sent out a request for people to submit their stories. The only uplifting part of these stories is that these hounds were saved and now live the best life they can. They aren't hungry. They aren't neglected. They aren't tied up. They aren't sleeping in an old barrel or on the ground. They have beds to sleep on, literally, as in their human's king size bed. And some humans sing lullabies to their sweet hounds. Now these coonhounds know love and kindness.

Do not neglect to show hospitality to strangers, for by this some have entertained angels without knowing it.

Hebrews 13:2

Many of these rescue angels have saved more than one coonhound at a time or throughout their lives. God bless them. I've left out their names just to keep their privacy from any monsters who might recognize the story and come back to claim the dogs they left for dead. I've also summarized some stories but haven't left out any important details. I'm sure these angels feel the same way I do about giving up our dear coonhounds. To quote Charlton Heston, "From my cold, dead hands…"

Here goes. You might need to take a break and walk around, get more tissues to wipe your eyes, pray, get a drink (water, Coke, or something stronger), throw up. I had to take breaks while writing this. Some of the rescuers provided photos of their dogs when they rescued them; photos of where the dogs were kept or dumped. They were brutal.

I've broken up these stories with scriptures and descriptions of various hounds, even though the breed is not always noted. Read these stories. Research these breeds. You will find a coonhound that will suit your needs. And steal your heart. I promise.

My Ellie was tied to a tree for the first year of her life in Tennessee and starved within hours of her death when she was saved. The vet said she had about two hours left to live. She was 35 lbs. underweight when we got her. Ruger was dumped at a kill shelter at 6 months in southern Illinois because he is gun shy. He was moved to a no kill shelter where he sat for 2-1/2 years before I found him. Lucy was a stray puppy at 3 months and found on the side of a highway in Tennessee. They are now spoiled brats who regularly take over the couch and our bed. We wouldn't have it any other way!

I found Sasha online at PetFinders. She was pushed out of a truck onto a highway in Tennessee. A man saw it, picked her up, and brought her to his vet. He was elderly and she was too big for him to handle. One of the vet techs was a foster and took her. The rest is history. I got her in 2015 at about a year old.

Sophie's parents were strays who stole our shoes off the porch and ate them. They had a litter of pups after we repeatedly tried to catch them. My 12-year-old son caught four of the puppies with his fishing net. We found homes for three of them. Sophie turned our "NO DOGS!" home into a "DOG ALLOWED" home. I've survived 14 months now! LOL!

We found this dog in the woods. He was skin and bones with every health issue known to pets. Animal Control brought him in to our local shelter. My husband saw him while we were there donating. He told me we weren't leaving him there. So we didn't. One year and 40 pounds later he sleeps every night on our bed and loves his three other dogs that are in the home. We named him Ruckus.

American English Coonhound: This energetic and intelligent dog evolved from English Foxhounds which were brought to the New World. It was bred to adapt to rougher terrain, hunting fox by day and raccoon by night. It shows an effortless trot and never appears to get tired. Quite similar to the Treeing Walker Coonhound, it can adopt both the "cold nose" trail (straddling an old track for hours to locate the animal that left it) or follow a scent fast in pursuit of a fresh, active trail. As a pet, it needs firm handling but in return will be a devoted companion and good guard dog. (17)

My coonie is half red tick and half pit bull. She came from a lawsuit the local pound had with a man. He had 30+ coonhounds and left them all outside on chains refusing to give them food or water because they are "hunting dogs." My boyfriend (before I was with him) rescued her and then had to rescue her again from parvo. She's now three years old and an a**hole.

My guy, Skeet, his sister and son were all tied to barrels outside on a Mennonite farm for their first year and a half of life, just like the dogs were tied up in *The Fox and The Hound*. A rescue convinced the farmers to let them take the three in. Skeet went to a foster home but they couldn't handle him. Skeet was with the rescue for another year and a half before I accidentally stumbled upon him. I can't imagine my life without him!

$$\text{C}\!\!\times\!\!\text{O}$$

My dog (no name mentioned) was a puppy factory for a hunter. She was kicked to the curb when she was all used up.

$$\text{C}\!\!\times\!\!\text{O}$$

When Hurricane Michael came through North Carolina my sweet Bailey girl was at a shelter there. Because it was headed straight for the shelter, they had to evacuate but could not take the animals. They made the horrible decision to start euthanizing them! A hound rescue group was able to get three hounds out, one of which was Bailey. Hours later the shelter was demolished by the storm.

A quick-to-follow, bright, loyal and good-natured hunter and companion, the Black and Tan pleases hunter and owner alike. Although he can be assertive, this is an obedient, watchful dog. Owners must be wary of grooming and exercise requirements. In order to keep the ears clean and infection-free, regular attention is a must. (18)

My Chance was found starving on the side of the road. Unfortunately, he was mistakenly placed with a woman who had a mild hoarding problem. She had approximately 12 dogs and a nephew who abused them. When Chance came to us, he didn't even know what a treat was. I placed a peanut butter Kong in front of him and he was completely flabbergasted. He spent the first month at our home shaking in the corner. We had to carry him outside because he wasn't leash trained.

Moulson was abandoned in the woods by his hunting owner because he was gun shy. Then he was picked up by a dog fighter and used as a bait dog before being rescued and dumped in a kill shelter in Kentucky. He was pulled just before being put to sleep and sent to Ohio Hound Rescue in Cincinnati. A family adopted him but returned him five days later because their kids were abusive. I drove 13 hours to pick him up and it's been one of the best decisions ever!

Our Stella was born in South Carolina and was the only survivor of her litter. Her rescuer was unable to find her a foster in the south because she's a hound. She and her mom were strays and were both brought to New York to evacuate during Hurricane Florence. We wanted to rescue another dog to be a confidant companion to our Moulson. Her foster mom was only 45 minutes away from us and the second she hopped out of the car we were in love with her! Stella has brought so much spunk, craziness, laughter and love into our lives.

Jacee was dumped in the North Carolina woods. She was intact and had "stuff" pouring from her lady parts and was on the way to a uterine infection. She was also heart worm positive and underweight. She chose us at the shelter when we went looking for a Labrador. LOL. Now she is fat, spayed and healthy!

Cooper was found in a trash box on the side of the road. Two of his litter mates somehow got out and were hit by a car. Thank God my husband stopped to move their little bodies. Then we heard Cooper. And he's slept between us ever since.

A competitive and arduous sportsman, the Bluetick is the choice of many American hunters. It does remarkably well indoors and promises a fine companion and guardian to the family it loves. The breed's devotion to its family is only rivaled by its fervor on the field. (19)

Our Sweet Southern Belle came to us in Colorado from Northern Alabama. She was found with about 10 other dogs, dumped on the side of the road. The lady who first found and rescued them told me that Belle was one of a group of dogs found wandering in Lawrence County. Some backyard hunter breeders found out about them and tried to steal them from the shelter. The dogs were hidden and moved a few times. One of the fosters had to put hot wire with an alarm around their property to keep Belle from being bred to death in a tiny kennel. The dogs were moved from county to county until they could be moved out of Alabama. It was nuts. Belle is now safe, happy and so very loved at her furever home in NE Colorado!

Copper was left outside in Wisconsin in the Polar Vortex in January (-50 degrees). He was underweight, had fleas, and was aggressive and constantly biting his new parent. After four weeks Copper began gaining weight and a behaviorist works with him. His biting is getting better and TODAY he was able to go to Puppy Daycare and showed no signs of aggression towards anyone or any dog. It's been a huge day for us today!

My girl was found on top of a mountain in West Virginia with a trap on her back leg. She came up from WV as a foster. But you know what happens when you foster. I failed and now she is all mine and having the best life she could have. Her name is Miss Trapper Tripod! Trap for short.

Zcaro was kept in a crate 24 hours a day that was too small. He was starved and abused. My son's girlfriend brought him to live with us. We kept him and got rid of her. Now Zcaro is rotten after two years with us.

Rescue me, O LORD, from evil men;
preserve me from violent men who devise evil
things in their hearts.

Psalm 140:1-2

My girl was a 14-week-old puppy and had an accident in the house. The male owner was playing video games and was so angered by her that he picked her up above his head and slammed her into her mess multiple times. Her right rear femur snapped in half. The local impound where I work was contacted about the incident. The police got involved and the owners surrendered the puppy over to the impound.

The puppy was transported to the U of M, where surgery was performed to save her leg. She now has two plates and nine screws. I fostered her during her recovery with absolutely no intentions of adopting, and well, now I can't imagine life without a coonhound. She has made a full recovery and now lives life to the fullest.

The owner was prosecuted to the fullest extent, thanks to our awesome courts and support from the community to pursue pressing charges.

Our Jacob was found on the streets of Alabama as a tiny pup. Someone had tossed him out. He was malnourished, had rickets and was at death's door. A vet tech found him and brought him to work with her. The clinic nursed him back to health. A rescue organization here in Maine got him and fostered him until he was fully recovered and ready to be adopted. Jacob is still pigeon-toed from the rickets and had to have major leg surgery. But he's been with us for five years!

Jasper was found as a stray pup in northern Maine. The rescuer thinks he had been dumped because he was healthy, trained and happy. Apparently, a lot of hound dumping goes on when they don't hunt well. Jasper's been with us since last August and is our 10-year-old's best buddy.

(Note: Jasper and Jacob are now brothers.)

I adopted my tripod, Pi, after the local SPCA brought her to the vet clinic where I work. Her leg was badly broken and her knee was damaged. Her owners had no explanation as to how it happened, just that she got lost and when she came home it was like that. They surrendered her because they didn't want to pay to have her leg treated. Pi's leg was amputated and I took her home to recover. She never left. That was 18 months ago.

The strong desire to fulfill his master's wishes and his even stronger ability to do so have made the Redbone an extensively used hunter. With the thrusting grit of a terrier and the pumping stamina of a husky, the Redbone is every hunter's hot-trailed dream come true. In the home, he is affectionate and kind. (20)

Copper was brought home from the shelter when he was five months old. He was in the shelter with his brother. They were from Texas. The brother gave me no eye contact and couldn't care less. Copper, my boy, on the other hand jumped in my lap and put his arms around me and wouldn't let go! I knew he was going home with me.

His brother was adopted out four times and brought back due to very bad aggression towards people and dogs. It was so sad. Copper has some issues but we have overcome most of them and he is now a therapy dog. I had a coonie when I was young and I always said I wanted another one before I died. Copper may be the one who puts me in the grave, but I'll be smiling!

I wish I could say Copper's brother had a happy ending but he had to be euthanized. It takes a lot of work and lots of patience when a dog has issues. Luckily, I have both, and so much love.

We didn't see a tail wag from Ruger for two solid weeks after we brought him home. He didn't trust people. He was adopted, sent to a shelter, adopted again, and returned again. His behavior was so poor (he was three years old) when I got him that the shelter called me a month after I adopted him and asked when I was bringing him back! I was confused as to why they would call and ask that. "Because no one wants this dog," was the reply. That broke my heart. Ruger is my love.

Chi was from West Virginia. She was starved, beaten, burned, branded and kept in a crate. She did not get any exercise and was shocked each time she made a sound for THREE-AND-A-HALF YEARS because she would not hunt. I got her 11 months ago when her bones were sticking out and all she did was pace for a week without eating or drinking. She was so fearful. Eventually she ate and I fed her many meals during the day so she could gain weight. This caused her to develop stomach problems. She eats four half-cups each day because if she's left more than four hours without food, she vomits up her first meal. She gets pumpkin, blueberries, strawberries, peanut butter, yogurt, green beans, celery, and tomatoes as treats, along with Milk Bones.

Chi was weaned off Prozac but is still very fearful of outdoors. She will not walk on a leash without issues, such as pulling me down. I've been using a trainer to help us. I rescued a kitten and Chi's scared of it. She will get used to it because she gets along with my other cat. I love her so much and I've given her ALL of my time, never leaving her unless it's to go to the store or an appointment. She sleeps in bed with me all coonied up under a blanket. She's gained weight and is absolutely gorgeous!

My husband surprised me with a puppy for my birthday. We were told they were "cattle dogs" so I started researching. When I went to pick out my puppy, we saw six of the most adorable little girls on the planet. They were NOT cattle dogs! I had no idea what they were but I picked my Journey. The conditions appalled me. No food or water. The puppies were kept in a tiny pen that they kept escaping from. They lived on a high traffic highway. There was another dog tied to a tree. We went to the store and bought some dog food and went back and fed and watered all of the dogs.

The next day, after not sleeping a wink, my husband called me and said he couldn't stand the thought of those dogs getting out and getting killed on the highway. We talked about it and he went and got the rest of them! We already had five rescue dogs. My daughter took one. We still have five: Journey, Harper, Magic, Anya and Georgie Girl. They have totally destroyed my house but I love them all so very much.

Plott Hound: The breed's "all-in-the-family" background makes it a fine companion. Southern owners report that

they are quick to learn, quick to trail, and quick to love. Their personable natures are surely not evident on the trail. The courage and tenacity to play chicken with a 500-pound papa bear or a ticked-off boar are enviable. (21)

My girl, Tress, was found in the woods. She was skin and bones, heart worm positive and her foot pads were bleeding. Her owner had brought her to a no-kill shelter in Louisiana. Tress had a high fever and the veterinarians didn't think she would make it. They put out a plea for a foster and I went and got her. I foster failed and two years later she is happy and healthy.

I was taking a drive one Saturday and cut across this dirt road to head to the grocery store in Sandstone, MN. I saw a donkey and stopped to take a picture of it. I heard dogs howling and 20 feet ahead of me was the property where the dogs were. At first, I thought there were 15-20 dogs; turned out there were over 70.

(A photo was included with this story. Coonhounds were chained to old barrels. The ground was mud and there was junk all around them. They had no food or water. A dog at the top of the photo was looking to the right, over a hill where more dogs were chained up; where the "real hell" was.)

Thanks to my consistent posting on Facebook and repeated pressure on the powers that be, he voluntarily turned his dogs over to the shelter. I adopted the two oldest dogs, Roy and Patch. However, Patch wasn't old.

My Treeing Walker Coonhound was taken to the vet at 9 weeks old to be put to sleep because her leg had been "accidentally" broken. The vet refused to euthanize her and took her to the animal shelter. We adopted her, broken leg and all. She healed within two weeks.

Emmylou was used as a puppy factory. She was dumped at the shelter at the age of 3-1/2, allegedly right after weaning 13 puppies. The veterinarian guessed that Emmylou had probably had five or six litters. The shelter posted a photo of her the very first day she arrived. I was there when they opened the next morning. A special needs foster mom nursed her back to life for 6 weeks until she was strong enough and healthy enough to spay. I was able to visit her and introduce her to the dog we had. She was terrified of me, and that lasted for a very long time. Emmylou joined our family and I was convinced she had never been indoors before.

...But he who is gracious to the needy honors Him.

Proverbs 14:31b

I adopted my Stormy in June. Two years ago, she was taken from a puppy mill and dumped at a rural shelter. She was pregnant. Another shelter pulled her from the shelter where she was dumped. Stormy gave birth to 14 puppies.

The first person to adopt her returned Stormy to the shelter. The second person to adopt her abandoned her in the local city. She was microchipped and had tags so when the owners were contacted, they said they had moved and couldn't take her with them. The shelter has a contract that states you are to bring the dog back to them 24/7 if you can't keep them during their lives. The third person who adopted her also returned her.

I am the fourth, and LAST, person to adopt her! When I met Stormy, she was 39 pounds and very terrified. Today she weighs 57 pounds, runs four mornings/week with me and is very gentle with everyone. She's picky about other dogs but that doesn't bother me. She has the sweetest personality.

On October 8, 2011, I rescued Dempsey, my best friend. On that day, I had no idea that he would be the one rescuing me. He had come from a terrible place where he was kenneled all of the time. He was 33% underweight and terrified of everything, mostly men. I could tell he had been beaten and that his spirit was broken. From that very first night when I picked him up and put him on my bed, he totally bonded with me.

I was not in a good place myself. My spirit was broken, too. My daughter had passed away on January 28, 2010. Then, Jazmyn, my black lab, died seven weeks later. Cassidy, my yellow lab, died 11 months later. I was hurting in a big way and isolating myself. We went to the shelter so I could look at a couple of female labs who were available for adoption. We told a volunteer a little bit about what was going on and how our little Yorkshire "terrorist" did not like other dogs. The volunteer mentioned another dog that I had not seen on the website. He was a male and I was look-ing for a female. But I told her, "Bring him out for me." He was a three-year-old Treeing Walker Coonhound. I knew very little about this breed. The poor thing looked like a goat with his "hang dog" look and long droopy ears and sad, sad eyes. When I looked into his eyes, I felt like I was looking into a mirror. Dempsey needed help. He needed to know he could trust people. He needed to know that he would not be hurt again. He needed ME! And I so, so needed HIM!

Dempsey is so sweet and loving. He is a perfect companion. I began getting out of the house and going to dog parks to socialize him. In turn, I was socializing again. We are the best of friends.

If you are considering getting a dog, please, please go to your local animal shelter or rescue. You will not be disappointed. Don't overlook a shy, somewhat withdrawn dog. These are the ones that would do anything to please you and will always stay by your side. REMEMBER—that dog could be rescuing YOU!

Not a coonhound, but…I have a German Shorthair Pointer who was absolutely terrified when we got him. He was terrified to the point that he would actually lose control of his bowels out of sheer fear if someone approached him. It was over a year before he finally wagged his stubby little tail. I bawled my eyes out when it happened!

Eight years later he's my best buddy and has become my "foster dog welcome wagon." He greets each new foster dog with love, patience and play until they realize it is safe. It's truly awe-inspiring to earn the trust of a terrified dog.

I found my Bella on PetFinders along with a Dalmatian I was interested in. I met Simon the Dalmatian first and decided to add him to my pack. I became a monthly sponsor for Bella at her rescue. Three years later she was still there, waiting for a home. I decided four dogs couldn't be much harder than three and brought her home. Bella was my first coonie. She and Simon hated each other until the day he died. Bella kicked his butt regularly, but he mostly deserved it. We lost Bella a couple of years ago.

Minnie Mouse was returned three times by folks who did not understand hound behavior. She was beaten for chewing and became very nervous. Minnie was also allowed to whine endlessly by another family and not trained to understand her place in the pack. She was a nightmare when we first brought her home but with time and love, she came around. She is still very stubborn and willful but she is much better. Minnie also has issues with being jealous but a trainer has helped us with that. Minnie loves her sister and has a heart of gold. Her barking is unbearable but her smile is priceless.

Freddie was a research dog at a university in upstate New York. I adopted him in October and I am quite sure he spent the first three years of his life in a cage. He was terrified of everything, didn't understand how to walk on a leash, wouldn't eat or drink out of a bowl, didn't know how to go up steps, wasn't food motivated and didn't even know how to sit, and didn't make a peep until January (he barked and scared the crap out of himself!). He has come so far in the past four months. He eats and drinks out of his bowls, walks nicely (most of the time) on his leash, has mastered the outdoor steps, now loves treats and will sit on command, is doing well on house training, and I know now he

CAN bark if he tries, which I wasn't sure of before. I'm so thankful I found him!

Do not let kindness and truth leave you; bind them around your neck, write them on the tablet of your heart. So you will find favor and good repute in the sight of God and man.

Proverbs 3:3-4

Today is Bo's first Gotcha Day! He started out as a foster I did not plan on keeping. No one wanted an older, intact, outside hound, including me. Knowing his history, I could not help but feel sorry for him. His first 9 years were spent on a farm, mostly chained and in deplorable conditions. He has broken teeth from trying to free himself. His former owner became an alcoholic/drug addict and went to jail. Two other dogs had died feet from Bo. One froze to death; the body was there for weeks. The other was attacked and killed by a bobcat. Many other animals died on that farm also. I can only imagine the smell of death that was in the air. Bo was often without fresh food or water his last two years on that farm. There were times his life was absolutely horrific. I had heard about how his life was for the years previous to us getting him. It is a miracle he is even alive. It was upsetting that I could not do anything about it then. He was not my dog. Like I stated, I never had planned on keeping him. However, I looked into his soulful brown eyes, thought about what an uncertain future he would have if I did not keep him. I could not bear it. He is such a sweet boy...and deserves the best life I can possibly give him every day, for the rest of his life.

Hi Coonie pals! I have kind of a sad question…have any of y'all rescued pups with birdshot in them? I rescued Rooster 10 months ago, he was 8 months old. The shelter had him for two months prior to my rescuing him. I was told they got all the pellets out besides the one on his head because it would cause more harm than good. However, his body still rejects pellets all the time. Maybe one or two pellets a month. They don't bother him until they're about to come out of his skin. Then he won't let me touch them and he constantly licks it. I was just wondering if anyone had an idea how much longer this will last?

Ember still has buckshot or bb's in her chest and side.

Blue has 25 or so in him. They don't seem to cause him any problems, and his body has never expelled any of them. What kills me is that he was about 10 months old when he went into rescue, and he didn't have any obvious injuries then, so someone shot at him when he was a pretty young pup!

Do you get it? If you're not bawling, or at least teary-eyed, or maybe even somewhat nauseous, re-read this chapter. Get angry about how dogs are just considered trash or disposable. Then tell God thank you for the angels who rescued these dogs from their living hell.

These are just a *few* of the cruelty/neglect/abandonment cases that occur with coonhounds. I shudder to think of what else is happening. If this book makes just one person aware of what is happening to coonhounds all over the United States, then hopefully that person will save at least one coonhound.

Is it possible to save all of the coonhounds and dogs being abused? Probably not. Awareness and action are the keys.

But with God, all things are possible. He tells us that!

...with God all things are possible.

Matthew 19:26

Chapter 14

The Coonhound Cemetery

N ot everyone who owns a coonhound is cruel to them. While it seems that many people who have coonhounds seem to discard them like trash or abuse them, there are decent humans besides rescuers who love their coonhounds.

In the movie *Sweet Home Alabama*, Jake and Melanie visit the grave of their bloodhound in a coonhound cemetery. To me, it's a very touching scene. And that got me wondering. Is there really a cemetery for hound dogs? I had heard once that there was. So, I looked it up. Sure enough, there *is* a coonhound cemetery.

The Key Underwood Coon Dog Memorial Graveyard is a one-of-a-kind cemetery. It is located at 4945 Coondog Cemetery Road in Cherokee, Alabama 35616.

The cemetery was founded on September 4, 1937, when Key Underwood buried his faithful hunting coonhound, Troop, at the hunting camp where they met regularly for 15 years to hunt raccoons.

Troop was considered the best hunting dog around. He was half Redbone coonhound and half Birdsong.

I had to research what a Birdsong hound is. The breed wasn't listed in the two dog books I referenced. So, I went to the internet. The closest reference I could find was an article, "History of the July Hound" by Rodney Sweat, which used information taken from *American Foxhunting: An Endangered Sport* by Sara Strahan.

In 1803, a foxhunter named Col. Myles G. Harris, from Georgia, went on a foxhunt with a mule trader named Ben Robinson of Mt. Sterling, Kentucky. They used hounds bred by Nimrod Gosnell of Maryland. Col. Harris was so impressed with Gosnell's hounds that he tried to buy a pair from him.

Gosnell decided to send Col. Harris a pair of pups, but when they arrived, they were wooly, tan, cock-eared pups. They arrived in July, so the male was named July. The female was named Mary. The pups were a laughingstock with the other hunters.

Col. Harris did not appreciate people making fun of his dogs so he moved them several miles away to his other farm where they were cared for by one of his slaves.

In 1859, July and Mary went on their first fox hunt with the other choice local hounds, whom Col. Harris invited to the hunt. July and Mary were the only two hounds who stayed with the fox; the other hounds scattered and gave out. July and Mary were not ridiculed again.

When Mary came into season, she was put in the gin loft, but jumped through a window and accidentally hanged herself. July became a stud in very high demand.

Col. Harris, who was developing hearing and sight problems, sent July and six other hounds to Putnam County, Georgia. He designated that the six hounds would be owned in common by his friends to make suitable crosses. He stipulated that July was simply loaned out and his title would remain with Col. Harris. Eventually, Col. Harris gave ownership of July to a Colonel Larry F. Birdsong and breeding privileges to other hounds to enhance July's offspring.

July was bred to hounds owned by Dr. Thomas Henry, hounds whose ancestors came from Ireland and bred to dogs in various kennels, eventually being crossed with hounds bred by Nimrod Gosnell and Dr. James A. Buchanan. Col. Birdsong crossed the Henry hounds with July and hounds descended from July, producing running hounds.

Although records of breeding were destroyed in a fire in 1929, Col. Birdsong is known as the father of the pedigree, the Birdsong hound, now known as the July Hound. His hounds became the standard for all foxhounds in America. The hounds had a characteristic curl of hair on the shoulder, contributed by the Henry hounds. In 1903, these dogs became known as the English Coonhound by the United Kennel Club.

Back to the coonhound cemetery, after that brief history lesson.

Troop was born April 1, 1922. He passed away September 4, 1937. Underwood knew the hunting camp, nestled in the Freedom Hills near Tuscumbia, was the only place where Troop could rest. Troop loved the camp.

On Labor Day weekend, Troop was placed in a cotton pick sack and placed three feet down into the ground. A chimney brick became his grave marker. Underwood (I would love it if I discovered that I was related to Key Underwood, since that is my maiden name) used a hammer and screwdriver to chisel Troop's name and the date. A special marker has since been erected in memory of Troop.

So the Key Underwood Coon Dog Memorial Graveyard came into existence. Soon other coonhound owners began laying their beloved hounds to rest here. Today, there are more than 300 dogs buried in this graveyard. There is not another graveyard like it anywhere in the world.

In a 1985 interview, Underwood stated, "When I buried Troop, I had no intention of establishing a coon dog cemetery. I merely wanted to do something special for a special coon dog."

When asked why other kinds of dogs weren't allowed to be buried at the cemetery, Underwood said, "You must not know much about coon hunters and their dogs, if you think we would contaminate this burial place with poodles and lap dogs."

Stipulations for coonhounds that can be buried in the Key Underwood Cemetery are that the owner must claim their pet is an authentic coon dog, a witness must declare the deceased is a coon dog, and a member of the Key Underwood Coon Dog Memorial Graveyard, Inc., must be allowed to view the coonhound and declare it as such.

I had hoped to visit the cemetery to see it for myself and do some research for this book. But due to the Covid-19 virus, I have not been able to travel to this cemetery. So, as I noted earlier, my research was done on the internet. I also found YouTube videos. If you are unable to actually visit the Key Underwood Coon Dog Memorial Graveyard, I highly recommend checking out videos on YouTube.

Watching the videos is pretty fascinating. And it brought tears to my eyes. These hounds were well-loved. The grave markers range from simple stones, bricks, metal, or wood with the dog's name and dates of birth and death crudely etched or burned into it, to elaborate, custom-made granite gravestones. These gravestones include special epitaphs unique to the dog, accomplishments the dog made, such as Grand Champion, the dog's name, date of birth and death, and the owner's name. Some have a relief of a coonhound, engraved raccoon tracks, treed raccoons, brass plates, and coonhounds sleeping on top of the gravestone. Ages of the dogs range from 7 years to 18 years.

Some graves are outlined with bricks. Some contain flowers. Special tokens of the dogs' lives are placed on the grave or gravestone, such as their collars, leashes, and food bowls.

Many of these dogs, such as Troop, High Pocket, Loud, Queen, and Ranger (owned by E.T. Buck Jaynes, close to Jayne so I might have to investigate and see if there is a family relation) are legends. Hatton's Blue Flash and Hatton's Blue Flash, Jr., father and son, are both American Kennel Club and United Kennel Club Grand National Champions. Hunter's Famous Amos was Ralston Purina's Dog of the Year in 1984. I'm fairly certain that every dog buried here is a legend, if only in their master's eyes. And they aren't wrong.

There are also videos of funerals for certain coonhounds. They are well-attended, with some mourners bringing their beloved coonhounds with them to pay their respects.

Coonhounds from all across the United States are buried here. They don't have to be specifically from Alabama. There is also a big celebration on Labor Day honoring the coonhounds. American flags are placed on each grave. During the celebration, there are bands, dancing, food, and a liars contest ("storytelling").

More than 7,000 people visit this cemetery each year. I hope to make it 7,001.

Chapter 15

Nothing Is Ever Easy

In the spring of 2019, Casey began limping on his left front leg. We had to stop going on our evening walks because Casey really struggled, even on short walks.

We took him to our vet, and Dr. Strong treated it as inflammation. She said his left front foot looked like it was starting to turn out a little. Her German Shepherd had the same problem, but it didn't slow him down. We started Casey on anti-inflammatories, which seemed to help. At first. X-rays on his left front foot didn't reveal anything out of the ordinary. Perhaps it was from the countless times he bounded over the back of the couch. Who knows?

By August, he was limping pretty badly and his left shoulder was winging out. He started to lose muscle mass in that shoulder, too. We had the veterinarian who did Ajax's ACL surgeries, Dr. Eldridge, examine Casey. He ordered x-rays of his shoulder and neck, but they didn't show anything. Dr. Eldridge said the problem was probably neurological. Or the long shot was that something, a tumor, was pressing on his nerves, and an x-ray wouldn't show it. We would need an MRI.

My mom radar went off. Actually, my mom radar had gone off the second Casey began limping. Oh, how I wish I had listened to it. It couldn't possibly be a tumor.

I had a left hip replacement on September 4. Harry, my horse, had surgery for an ulcer in his left eye on September 9. Here's a *big* shout out to Courtney, with whom I board Harry, for taking him to the equine hospital and picking him up, and for giving him his meds while I was recuperating.

By now, Casey had really slowed down. He was struggling to walk. He also slept. A lot.

On Monday, September 16, he wouldn't get up. He wouldn't even try. He would eat treats, though. I managed to get down in the floor with him and sat with him all morning, crying and praying and telling this sweet coonhound how much I loved him.

David came home from work at noon. He started to cry, too. He is crazy about Casey. He picked up Casey and took him outside. When he set him down, Casey limped off and peed. He barked at something and trotted around a little bit. Then he was ready to come back in!

I sat on the couch, and David put Casey next to me. I spent the afternoon crying and petting Casey and telling him how much I loved him.

After a while I called Dr. Eldridge, and he suggested a CT scan, which would be cheaper than an MRI, but there was still the chance the MRI would pick up things the CT scan might miss. I scheduled an MRI at the emergency veterinary clinic, and it was scheduled for September 27. It was going to be at least $2,500, maybe more. Same with the Oklahoma State Veterinary School.

Dr. Eldridge called another veterinary surgeon, and she arranged for Casey to get an MRI at the equine hospital where Harry had had surgery. It was about half the cost of what the other places were going to be.

Casey got his MRI September 19. David dropped us off, and I stayed there all day. The MRI took several hours and then Casey had to recover. I occupied my time in the waiting room, reading horse magazines and walking around the parking lot with my cane and watching the veterinarians observe horses moving in the parking lot. When they brought Casey out, he was still groggy, so I sat in the floor with him until David picked us up.

The next day we got the results. They shook me to my core.

There was a tumor on Casey's C6-7 vertebrae. The tumor was pushing on his nerves and spine, causing him to limp and his shoulder to wing out, and that was also why he was losing muscle mass.

Casey has cancer.

Not my Casey. Not my Treeing Walker Coonhound who has been through so much in his life. No. It's not fair. Not at all.

Dr. Eldridge and the spinal surgeon were very iffy about surgery for Casey. The tumor was pressing close to his bone, so we couldn't even do a needle biopsy. If I wanted a biopsy, it would have to be done surgically. And there was so much nerve damage, Casey would have to have his left front leg amputated, but there could also be much more nerve damage done trying to remove the tumor. There could also be more tumors along his spine. We only had an MRI done on his neck.

I was a wreck. Dr. Eldridge, God love him, told me not to throw in the towel yet. Steroids would help with the edema around the tumor. They could have long-term effects, but we could worry about those later.

David began giving Casey steroid and peptide injections. We also started Casey on fenbendazole, a dog wormer, combined with CBD oil, curcumin, and vitamin E.

Why dog wormer?

Joe Tibbens is from Oklahoma. He was diagnosed with small cell lung cancer. He went through chemo and radiation at M.D. Anderson. His cancer spread. The doctors told him to go home and call hospice as he just had weeks to live.

Joe was put on a drug trial at M.D. Anderson, which would maybe buy him some time; maybe a year, two tops.

However, his large animal veterinarian friend in western Oklahoma told him to try dog wormer, three days on and four days off. With nothing to lose, Joe started the dog wormer.

At the end of his trial, he received another scan. His tumors were gone! He was the only one in the trial with a clear scan. That's when he told the doctors about the dog wormer.

Listen to Joe's story on Wellness-Speaks.com. It is incredible.

With nothing for us to lose, we started Casey on fenbendazole. I was filled with hope. I prayed for Casey so much.

At night, since Casey couldn't hop up in my chair with me anymore, I would sit on the couch. Sometimes he would crawl up with me. Other times David would help Casey onto the couch by lifting his back end up so he could snuggle with Mom. Casey peed on the couch a few times. The couch that no dogs were allowed on. The couch that no dogs were allowed on that had a big rip in the cushions, because a certain dog whom I love very much, leaped over it repeatedly. That same couch was now being peed on. I simply wiped up the pee, sprayed Sol-U-Mel on it for odor, and let it dry. Casey couldn't control himself. We can always get another couch. I just flat didn't care.

Nothing is ever easy, right? No. It's not. Certainly not at Casa Jayne. Things weren't getting easier.

David has had repeated surgeries on his left foot due to ulcers caused by his metatarsals pressing down. He's had two metatarsals trimmed down, had a screw put in, had the screw removed because he was allergic to the metal, and then developed another ulcer in July from walking around Washington, D.C. So as soon as I got my three-week clearance to drive, David scheduled another foot surgery (September 26) to remove his sesamoid bone and trim the other metatarsals.

This is his last shot at his foot healing. But bless his heart, even though he shouldn't lift extra weight, he would pick Casey up to take him outside, adding 60 extra pounds to a foot he's trying to heal.

And then he told me he couldn't do it anymore. I understand. I was still on my 10-pound weight lifting limit. Coonhounds weigh more than 10 pounds.

We decided to board Casey at the vet for a few days, so I took him on October 3. My sisters and I were moving my mom from her crappy memory care facility to the nursing home in Okemah on October 5. Because we needed another crisis, causing our new mantra of "Nothing is ever easy" to be proven yet again. To be hammered into our skulls.

I kept my friends apprised of Casey's situation with Facebook posts. I asked for prayers, and so many of my friends included Casey in their prayers.

Right before a noon yoga class was about to begin, Leslie, a friend, asked me how Casey was doing. I shook my head and Leslie apologized. I quickly told everyone to lie on their backs to stretch while I wiped away the tears sliding down my face. I muddled through that class somehow without absolutely bursting into tears.

That night, at my 5:30 class, Kathryn, another friend was telling me about her new rescue dog. I asked what kind of dog it was.

"A Treeing Walker Coonhound," she proudly answered.

Gulp.

Then Melinda, a fellow dog lover (there are lots of dog lovers in my yoga classes) and labradoodle rescuer asked me how Casey was. I shook my head and history repeated itself.

After class, Melinda came up to me and apologized. I burst into tears and left. She explained everything to Kathryn and Kristen. Kristen loves dogs, too. Dog lovers get it.

I visited Casey at the vet on Thursday and Friday. He appeared to be getting around a little better. Dr. Eldridge agreed. I had some hope. There's *always* hope. Never ever forget that.

Casey and I hung out together in an exam room or outside in a dog run, where Casey would bark and sniff and walk around, then come and lie next to me. Casey had a lot of trouble getting up and down, but when it was time to leave, Casey tried to follow me. He wanted to go home.

Our problem at home was the hard-wood floors. If we could find a way for Casey to walk without falling, maybe *something* would be easy. Melinda had just lost her mother to cancer. Her mother's labradoodle, Jake, had passed away a few weeks earlier. He had some doggie grippy booties, so Melinda gave them to me. I also bought a bunch of yoga mats and unrolled them in our living room and bedroom, making a nice, non-slip path for Casey.

I brought Casey home on Monday, October 7. On the way home, I drove through Chick-Fil-A and got a 12-pack of nuggets. I pulled over and parked. I ate a couple of nuggets and gave my Casey the rest. He was so happy!

"Are dees all for me, Mama?" he seemed to say.

Casey ate his nuggets and looked at me with the biggest grin on his face. Yes, dogs grin. Dog people know this. I loved watching Casey eat his chicken nuggets and took some precious photos of him enjoying his treat.

Dr. Eldridge switched Casey to prednisone instead of the steroid injections. Steroids make you drink water. And pee. My surgeon had given me a steroid-injection prior to my hip replacement. For three nights post-surgery, I got up literally every hour to pee. It helped me master the walker, sitting down and standing up, let me tell you.

It affected Casey the same way. But with his booties, he could get up a little easier. Casey slept on one of the dog beds in our bedroom. I moved it closer to the sun room, and every hour we got up so he could go out and pee and then tank up on water.

Wednesday, October 9, marked the 24th anniversary of Daddy dying and going to heaven. Although it's gotten a little easier, it's always a day when he's ever-present.

It was a beautiful fall day, so I put Casey and Ajax outside while I went to teach my noon yoga class. I like Wednesdays because I just have the noon class and then one at 5:30 p.m.

When I got home Casey and Ajax sang me a song. A beautiful song, as all hound dog songs are. I stayed on the patio with them. A while later both dogs jumped up and ran to the east side of the house. Casey actually ran! It was a gimpy run, but he was running and barking. The Cox cable man was out front, so Casey was protecting me.

I left to go teach my 5:30 class. Since I felt much better, I asked Kathryn about her new coonhound. His name is Jack. He was found dumped and starving in Alabama and brought to a hound rescue in Oklahoma City. She showed me photos of beautiful Jack, and I told her Casey seemed to be better, and that I was just glad he was with me.

After class, I hurried home because Justin came home that evening to see Casey, and we had pizza. Justin had to help Casey outside to pee. But when Casey came in, he made a beeline for his bed in the study room at the front of the house.

Casey was eyeing us from his bed while we ate. Usually he's right next to someone at the table. But he stayed in his bed and watched us, wagging his tail whenever we looked at him. I took Justin's plate of pizza crust bones to Casey, and he gobbled them up. We had a nice visit with Justin and Casey did, too.

After Justin left, Casey moved to the dog bed in the living room. I went to take a shower. I was going to try and sleep a little bit before the nightly, hourly excursions to pee began.

I had just gotten into bed when Casey started barking. It wasn't a "there's somebody outside bark" or a bark I mentioned in Chapter 10. It was kind of a choppy yip, but it had a different sound to it. A bark that I had never heard before. You know the sound puppies make before their eyes open and they are looking for their mama? This was like that, only it was a bark.

It was a _calling_. A calling to someone.

I got up and Casey stopped barking when I worked my way down on the floor next to him. _Casey was calling for me._ He wanted his mama. I know this.

David said Casey had peed on the dog bed because he couldn't get up. He put some towels under Casey on the dog bed. We put a dog sling under him that my friend Suzy, the dog lover from yoga, loaned me. We took Casey outside, and he staggered off to pee.

Casey started barking again. It was the same bark. David and I both went outside. Casey was in the grass behind the butterfly bush on the east side of the yard. He had fallen down. He couldn't get up. Not at all.

I gulped. David picked him up and carried him inside and put him on the dog bed. And then I went and got my pillow. I told David I was sleeping on the couch. We dragged Casey and the dog bed over between the couch and David's chair. I covered up with my blanket that had Casey's face on it that the boys got me for Christmas last year.

David dozed for a while and then went to bed. I hung my hand over and stroked Casey. I twirled one of his floppy ears. And I told him how much I loved him. Over and over and over. The tears fell like a waterfall. All night.

How I wished Casey was piled up with me on the couch. For two years, anytime I was on the couch, there was a Treeing Walker Coonhound pressed up against me or on top of me. This was how we spent our first few nights together.

Casey started to pant so I got his water bowl, and he drank and drank and drank. He drank three or four full bowls of water that night. He didn't try to get up to go pee.

I slept for about 20 minutes around 03:00. The rest of the time was spent leaned over Casey, talking to him, petting him, and telling him how much he was loved. I asked him if he remembered the first time we met and then told him the story. I asked him if he remembered our walks he loved to take, the snuggles we had, holding hands and paws. And I told him I loved him and he was the best dog. I told him I was so grateful God led us to each other. I apologized to him for the treatment he had before we rescued each other. I told him I wanted more time with him. I told him it wasn't fair.

Coonhounds are supposed to live for 15 or more years. Casey was about 8, maybe 9. He should still have years left to live. It's just not fair.

And then I began to pray. My prayers for healing for Casey that I'd been praying for months turned into asking God to just let Casey go to sleep and not wake up. Please. *Please. If it is Your will, God.*

It wasn't God's will.

I got up to go to the bathroom. Casey tried to get up to go with me. He just couldn't. He ended up sliding around to the edge of the dog bed and facing the other way. I helped him back up on the dog bed. He peed and I wiped it up as it ran off the dog bed and onto the floor. I gathered the towels and took them to the washing machine. Sweet Casey tried to get up and follow me. He just couldn't.

I sat down on the floor next to him. It was about 04:30. I sat by him until 06:00 and had to go to the bathroom. When I came back, Casey had tried again to follow me. Now he was on the floor. I sat back down next to him.

The human body is about 70% water. Mine had been considerably less over the past few weeks, and was dropping rapidly by the hour.

Sweet Casey still pushed his head under my hand when I took my hand away. He was lying on his left side so he would lift his right hind leg, like he always did. Submission? He didn't have to submit to me. Comfort? He knows he can be comfortable around Mom. Love? Yes. He loves me.

David got up and I started crying. Again. I don't think I had ever really stopped crying. And I knew what was going to have to happen.

The vet didn't open until 08:00. David texted his nurse and had her move his patients back. Family emergency. A couple of weeks ago, when I had thought Casey was leaving us, and I was crying my eyes out, David told me out of all of the dogs we've had, Casey was his favorite. He apologized to Ajax. Justin always told me that Casey was my favorite. I tried to deny it, but he just laughed. He told me I should change Casey's name to "Special."

I texted the boys and my sisters to let them know what was happening. It was one of the most difficult texts I've written. I also got subs for my yoga classes. And then I called the vet. I could barely get the words out, but the wonderful receptionist knew. I told her it had to be Dr. Eldridge. She told me to be there at 09:00.

So that's it? I only have a little over an hour left with my beloved Casey?

I got up and went to get dressed. Casey didn't call to me. He didn't try to get up, either. I threw on a pair of jeans and a long-sleeved tee shirt. And then I went back to be by Casey's side. I gave him another treat and he ate it. I snipped off a little bit of Casey's short hair and put it in a baggie.

Ajax was really quiet. He knew. We let him sniff Casey and tell him good-bye. And then it was time to leave. Oh, how I wished it wasn't.

David put down the back seat in our car. We put Casey onto some towels and slid him in. I laid next to him. No seatbelt. I didn't care. I stroked Casey the entire way to the vet, which was only a few miles away.

A vet tech met us at the door and helped David bring Casey into a room. The same room where I had had little Lucy put to sleep.

They gently laid Casey down on his left side on the floor. The vet tech closed the shades on the window and door of the exam room. I got down on the floor and laid next to him. Casey lifted his right hind leg.

Dr. Eldridge quietly entered the room. He assured us we were doing the right thing. Were we? I knew we were, but inside my heart that was breaking into pieces, I wondered. He gave Casey a sedative and said he would be back in about ten minutes.

So. This is really it.

Music was softly playing through the speakers in the clinic. It wasn't loud, but I could hear it. The only song I can remember playing was *Sugar, Sugar* by the Archies. I love that song. It's a happy song. It's on my "Happiness" playlist and also the 60s playlist I use for my core classes. But it didn't make me feel happy.

I clung to Casey. I stroked his beautiful head and his shoulder and traced the "swirly" he had on his right shoulder (left one, too) where the hair growing from two different directions met, forming a swirly. I twirled his ear and slid my hands down his side and legs. I held his paw. And I told my wonderful coonhound how much I loved him. I asked him if he remembered the first day we met, our walks, the treats, and the wonderful times we spent together. I thanked him for his beautiful songs. I wanted to hear one of those songs again.

The sedative didn't seem to be working. Casey should have drifted off to sleep, but he didn't. I bent over him and put my face on his face and kissed and kissed and kissed him while Dr. Eldridge gave him a little more sedative.

I wanted to scream out that I had changed my mind. That it wasn't time for Casey to go. That maybe he would get better. But I simply couldn't speak.

Casey looked up at me and then moved his head to see David. David talked to him and told him what a good boy he was. Casey moved his head up and down on the rug, from David to me, almost like he was nodding at us. I don't know if it was the drug causing that. I think he was looking at David and me for the last time, and he knew it, and he wanted to see us.

When Dr. Eldridge came back in with the drug that would send Casey over the Rainbow Bridge to heaven, I buried my face in Casey's and wept. I told him how much I loved him and that I would never ever forget him. I told him that I thanked God for him every day. I told him to find Daddy. I told him I knew that he would be waiting for me, and when I show up to heaven, he will be at the gate made out of pearls, singing me a welcome song and letting everyone know that I have arrived.

I lifted my head and Dr. Eldridge listened to Casey's heart. It had stopped.

"He's gone," Dr. Eldridge said softly. "I'm so very sorry." He shook David's hand and said Casey was a good dog. He patted me on the shoulder and left.

So, this was it. It's over. I hugged my sweet, sweet, beautiful boy for the last time. I didn't want to leave him. How could I?

But I did. Reluctantly. I got up and walked to the door with David. I turned around to look at my beautiful coonhound one last time, lying on the floor like he was asleep. Oh, how I wished he would hop up and sing. I told him good-bye and that I loved him one last time. And then we left and closed the door.

I cried all day. All. Day.

When it was time to go to bed, I was absolutely exhausted. I cried myself to sleep and then slept like a rock.

The next morning, I had to get up for work. But I started crying when I woke up. I managed to get ready for work and was doing okay until I was getting my weights and ball out for the core class I had to teach. Kay, a friend told me she was so very sorry about Casey and I burst into tears. She hugged me, and I muddled through that class and the yoga class I had to teach afterwards.

I knew as I headed home that I wouldn't get a song. But Ajax was there and we spent the afternoon hanging out together. I placed Casey's collar on my nightstand.

Ajax knew Casey was gone. I have never seen him mourn outright, but I know he misses Casey.

A couple of days later I had to get something off my nightstand and moved Casey's collar. Ajax was in the dog bed next to me and when he heard Casey's tags jingle, he jumped up and looked towards the door. *Casey's home!*

I sat down on the bed and began to cry. I petted Ajax and told him I was so sorry. He settled down when he realized Casey was not home.

Casey's dog bed was still in our closet. Ajax would follow me into the closet and lie in it, smelling the scent of his brother. I left it there for a couple of weeks. The sad, empty dog bed that used to hold a coonhound curled up in a tight ball. It has lots of Casey's shed hair in it.

I moved the dog bed over to the other side of the closet, in the corner on my side. I folded the pink Pendleton blanket, *Casey's* pink Pendleton blanket, and placed it in the dog bed. Then I took the jeans and shirt that I wore the last time I was with Casey, folded them, and put them in the dog bed on top of the blanket. I put his K9 University bandana in the dog bed with my clothes and the blanket.

Casey's dog food bowl and placemat were moved to the shelf on the patio. No more dinner dances with this bowl. I took the pillow with the hound with glasses that had been on the couch and put it on our bed. This was the only pillow that Casey ever bothered. I would find it throughout the house. It had a small hole in it, from a certain Treeing Walker Coonhound.

My birthday is on October 20, so my sister Jennifer got me a gift card to Hobby Lobby. I told her I wanted to get a shadow box for Casey's collar.

The veterinarian's office called a few days later and said Casey's ashes had been delivered and I could pick them up. I steeled myself and went to get them. I started crying and really let go when I got back in the truck. When I got home, I opened the sack and saw the wooden box with paw prints that I had picked out. My Casey was inside. I tucked the box in the bottom drawer of my nightstand. I looked at the clay impression of Casey's paw that they made and cried some more. I placed it next to him.

It's still hard to believe that Casey is gone. I only had him for two years, three months and 19 days. Not nearly long enough. I thank God I had him for that time. But it wasn't fair that the first years of his life were unkind, abusive, and cruel.

Casey was truly loved for those two years, three months, and 19 days. He was an absolute gift to our family for that brief moment of time. And such a blessing.

What if our paths had never crossed? Would Casey have starved to death on the streets? Or would he have survived long enough to suffer and die from cancer, paralyzed and unable to move from some hole he had crawled into for some semblance of shelter?

But our paths *did* cross. God saw to that. And He taught me how much I could love a dog and how awesome coonhounds are. Because without Casey, I never would have learned about the plight of coonhounds across America. I don't think I would have become as involved in rescuing dogs. Maybe I would have just continued to send ARLO a few bucks every now and then. I believe that God sending Casey to me was God calling me to help His dogs. To minister to His dogs.

I like to think that my Casey forgot most of what his previous life had been like and that he died knowing how much, how *very, very, very* much he was loved. And that we will be together again. And that he was a good boy. And that he was a good dog. And that he had a home. A home where he was loved. Probably his very first *home.*

June 21, 2020, was Casey's third "Gotcha Day." The day I found him and brought him home to be mine. The day Casey got a home. A family. A last name.

I got the box with his ashes out, unscrewed the bottom of the box, and opened it. When I lifted the black velvet bottom off of the box, there were the ashes. I knew they were there but it still took me by surprise. They were wrapped up neatly in a clear plastic bag secured with a zip tie. I looked at it for a minute or two, processing the fact that this was the remains of my beloved Casey. Then I snipped off the zip tie and took the little box outside.

I opened the plastic bag and took some of his ashes and spread them around the yard. I started at the south gate and sprinkled some there. This was where he stood and protected me and guarded his yard. I told him how much I missed him and loved him and thanked him for always standing guard to protect me. The area around this gate was worn down to the dirt, becoming mud when it rained. It got so bad that I had to put down a liner and cover it with rocks. Grass is growing over the rocks now. But now a little bit of Casey is there, forever a guardian at that gate.

Casey ran along the west, north and east fences, chasing the squirrels and deer and lawn men. I put some of his ashes there. Now he can always protect the perimeter of his home.

After Casey died, I found a footprint of his on the west side of the yard. I took a picture of it and cried and cried. I put some of his ashes there, too.

I put a few ashes by the butterfly bush on the east side of the yard, where Casey sat and stared into a tree, looking at a raccoon that no one but him could see, until I found it on the ground. I told him now he could always look for raccoons. It is also the place where Casey was in the yard for the very last time, where he called for his Mama and where David and I picked him up and brought him inside. Now part of him will be there forever. I told him I loved him so much.

The southeast corner of the yard, next to the gate to the purple bridge, was also a lookout point for Casey. I have a potted vegetable garden there. And now a part of Casey is there as well, guarding our yard from all vantage points.

The rest of Casey's ashes are sealed back up in the wooden box with paw prints on it. He's resting in the bottom drawer of my nightstand, next to his Mama.

When I die, I want to be cremated. I want the ashes of my pets, including my Casey, and some strands of Harry's tail (and any future horses I have) to be mixed with mine. That way, part of Casey will always be at the only home he ever knew, and the rest of him will be with the only Mama he ever knew.

Casey will always and forever be...

Special.

Chapter 16

Shark Bumping God

I was still in a fog. Sad. Depressed. Weepy. Little things sent me into tears. Watching television. Going to sleep. It didn't matter. David brought me a bag of Snickers Minis and handed them to me. I hugged him and just sobbed and sobbed.

Patty, a good friend, ordered a pair of socks with Casey's photo on them, hoping they would bring a smile to my face. They were shipped to David's clinic. He brought the box home and when I opened the box and saw those socks, I bawled like a baby.

A wonderful couple on LWMRC posted this:

> Ok guys…It's time to celebrate! This weekend we'll be doing our 9th Annual Tennis Ball Ride. 8 years ago we had to let our sweet Tucker go because the pain from the bone cancer was just too much. When we left the vet's office we were so sad. We did

not know what to do with ourselves. We decided to grab Tucker's tennis ball and go for a bike ride with it. We now celebrate yearly the amazing animals that we have loved and lost. We still have that same tennis ball that goes with us each year. We share stories and laugh and remember. Share with me your memories, your photos and your thoughts about those sweet souls that have touched your lives.

Well, of course I shared my Casey with them. And photos of my sweet boy. A few days later I got this response, causing the tears to flow once again. But I'm so grateful to these friends and how they honored Casey.

Ann Underwood Jayne thank you for sharing your sweet Casey with us. Those special dogs stay in your hearts forever. Today we rode and celebrated his memory.

By Sunday, I really wasn't better, but decided I needed to go to church anyway. Jennifer was there, as was our friend, Kathy, who hugged my neck and caused the tears to flow again.

Randy was preaching. I can't recall specifically what the sermon was about. All I know, and I wrote it down in the "Notes" section of my Bible, is that the Psalm Randy quoted was meant for me. A Psalm I needed to hear right then. A Psalm that will forever be a reminder to me about my precious Casey.

...And they will sing of the ways of the LORD.

Psalm 138:5

Sing. Casey sang to me. I thought of my dear sweet Casey, singing his beautiful song to God in heaven. The tears began to flow. But my heart got a little lighter because God knew what Randy was going to preach about. And He knew that I had to be there, that I needed to be comforted. So I just *knew*, right then, that Casey was in Heaven.

The next day, on Monday, October 14, 2019, a plea for help on the ARLO Volunteer Facebook page beckoned to me.

Remember Jack Walker? I told you about him in Chapter 6. ARLO rescued this poor, abused Treeing Walker Coonhound, got his wounds treated, neutered him and placed him in a wonderful foster home. Now he was coughing and needed to go to the vet. Wendell and Sheila, his foster parents, were both working and couldn't take him. I volunteered. Why not? I was finished with work at 1:00, so I could zip down and get him and take him to Henryetta to the vet.

I got to Wendell and Sheila's house. They were fostering two other dogs as well, a white dog named Alice and another Treeing Walker Coonhound named Bella.

Animal Control had picked up Bella and taken her to the pound. Her owners decided she wasn't worth saving. ARLO and I thought differently. I messaged Jaime and Misty, then sent them a check to pay for Bella's boarding until a foster home could be located. I was not about to let that girl be euthanized because her heartless owners didn't feel like she was worth saving.

Bella looked a lot like Casey. I gulped. She jumped up and put her big feet on my chest. I petted her and fought back tears. Jack Walker and Alice were barking at cats that were in the alley. But Jack Walker came over when he was called and laid down by Wendell. He rolled over on his back and I scratched his belly. He was mostly black and white with a brown head and ears, as well as a few brown spots on his back and rear legs.

Wendell helped me get Jack Walker to the car. He climbed in the front seat of our Lexus (the same car I brought Casey home in) without a problem. I was driving it since it was easier to get in and out of after my hip replacement. I could see the scars on his back legs where we believed he had been mauled as a bait dog.

Off we went. Jack Walker curled up in the front seat in a classic coonie curl. He went to sleep and let out a little whistle with every exhale. It was pretty cute.

About halfway to Henryetta, he raised his head and looked at me. He wagged his tail. He wasn't worried. Jack Walker seemed to trust me.

I saw that he had a cherry eye in his left eye. Poor guy. He's been through the wringer. I had to keep my eyes on the road, but I glanced over and noticed the hairless places on his front paws and back legs. Healthy pink skin was showing; skin that should be covered by hair. Above his right eye are two small hairless patches, possibly from a dog bite.

Jack Walker was looking at me, whistling. I reached over and patted him with my right hand. He laid his head on my hand and went back to sleep, softly whistling.

And my broken heart mended a little bit. Something started to fill in a crack or two.

When we got to the veterinarian's clinic, I got to see Dr. Lisa Coale, a friend I had grown up with and who also happened to be Dr. Tolleson's granddaughter. She told me how sorry she was to hear about Casey. Jack Walker stood between us, wagging his tail while she examined him. The vet tech came and got him and led him away. Well, she tried. Jack Walker didn't want to leave, but finally he did. Then Dr. Coale and I had a great visit.

On the drive home, I thought about Jack Walker. A lot.

I had been praying so hard to God, asking Him to get me through all of the things I was going through and to give Casey a hug. I told God I just knew that He and Casey would send another dog to me. Casey would tell God, "That one! That's the one! Mama will rescue and love that dog like she rescued and loved me."

A couple of days later, Jack Walker was able to go home. Wendell went and got him. Dr. Coale had started him on meds for his cough. She had removed his cherry eye and x-rayed Jack Walker to look at his lungs. She discovered that he had many buckshot pellets peppered throughout his body, some close to bones. Maybe the spots above his right eye are from buckshot. Whether they are from buckshot or animal bites, Jack Walker is lucky he didn't lose his eye.

Dr. Coale also tested Jack Walker for heart worms. Guess what? He was positive.

ARLO didn't have the money to pay for the fast-kill heart worm treatment. It's hard to adopt out dogs who are heart worm positive so a Facebook message for ARLO board members was sent out to see what we should do about Jack Walker. Was euthanasia the only answer?

I texted Misty and Jaime. I would adopt Jack Walker. Did I check with David? No. Was I ready for another coonhound? I don't know. I suppose so. Regardless if I was ready or not, this dog needed me.

And then I realized that Casey had been shark bumping God.

"This is the one, God! He needs my Mama."

God and Casey had found a dog for me. A coonhound who had been shot and chewed up and left shut up in a shed without food or water. Left to die. Discarded. Rubbish. Broken.

Look upon my affliction and rescue me...

Psalm 119:153a

Would they let me adopt Jack Walker? I told them I had done the slow-kill monthly heartworm treatment with Casey, and he was clear in six months. I was told that if I adopted Jack Walker, I could do whatever treatment I wanted on him! I was approved immediately, even though I went through the formality of filling out an adoption application and wrote out my check for Jack Walker's adoption fee, plus a little extra to help with his vet bill.

On Saturday, October 19, I got up to go to Okemah. I was going to visit Mama in the nursing home. Jennifer and Rachel went with me. I was also going to bring Jack Walker home.

I still hadn't told David.

So right before I left, I mean *right before* I left, I told David I was bringing Jack Walker home. I told him he needed a home and care, that he had been shot and attacked. I said he would be my birthday present, which was tomorrow.

David simply asked me if I thought it was too soon to get another dog. I shook my head no, stood up, and left before he could say anything else.

We visited Mama and then went to Valerie's house. I was scheduled to get Jack Walker around 3:00, so Rachel went with me. Wendell and Sheila gave him lots of hugs and told him they loved him and to be a good boy. I thanked Wendell and Sheila for taking such great care of Jack Walker. I promised them I'd take wonderful care of him and post lots of photos so they could keep up with him. (FYI, I have kept that part of the bargain. I've posted *tons* of photos of him!) Jack Walker got in the back seat, and we left.

When we got to Valerie's, Jack Walker hopped out and greeted everyone with a tail wag. He loved Camden and Cale, let them pet him, and wasn't fazed by Valerie's barking dogs. He was going to be all right!

On the way back to Edmond, Rachel rode in the back seat with Jack Walker. He slept all the way back with his head in her lap.

I had told Ian and Justin about Jack Walker. Justin thought having a Jack and an Ajax might be confusing, so I told the boys we could rename him. Justin said he wanted to be included in the naming process, so I told him to start thinking of names. He mentioned one name but I nixed it. I can't even remember what it was.

Then he texted, "What about Bowie?" As in David Bowie. Ian and I agreed that Bowie would be a great name.

Bowie it is. Bowie Jayne.

Bowie, the Treeing Walker Coonhound formerly known as Jack Walker, greeted David with a tail wag and sniff. I think David's heart melted a little, too.

Justin came home the next day and met Bowie. Bowie immediately warmed up to Justin. He liked Ajax, too, although Ajax was a bit put off. I know he still missed Casey. But I think he was happy to have another dog around. We took the dogs for a walk and it was then, after looking at pictures I'd taken of Bowie, that I noticed that he has a black heart-shaped spot on his right rear hip and flank.

Of course, I posted them on Facebook. Many people told me that Bowie had hit the Doggie Lottery like Casey had. Several people noticed the heart. They all knew how much I was grieving for Casey. I was comforted very much when they told me that Bowie was stamped by Casey. I believe it. Casey had a little white heart on his black saddle. It's only fitting that he sent me a dog with a heart.

My good friend, Cheryl, asked me if I thought that maybe God had taken Casey because He knew that Bowie needed a home. I told her I think so. God works in mysterious ways; way beyond our limited thinking.

Bowie slept in his dog bed by my bed the first couple of nights. He wasn't housebroken, so he had to mark a few things. But he's smart and figured it out. Mostly.

We have slipped and called him Casey a few times. And my eyes fill with tears.

But you just can't help but be happy around Bowie. He is about four years old. He has quite a bit of energy but can also sleep and snore with the best of them. Toys are fun to play with and, of course, as any coonhound knows, it's also great fun to run around the yard and bark at nothing or at things that roamed around in the yard at night.

Bowie is still on medicines for his cough, so I took him to my veterinarian to be examined. And also so they could meet Bowie.

Dr. Eldridge put Bowie on a monthly heart worm treatment and then x-rayed his lungs to see if he had any damage to them from being shot or mistreated, which might explain Bowie's cigarette-hacking cough. His lungs did have damage, but it was due to the intense heartworm infestation he had. The larvae had whittled and carved their way through his lungs, so he was put on prednisone to help with his cough. And Benadryl. The medicines are easy for Bowie to take because David makes Bowie buttered toast every morning and warm, buttered toast is a good way to hide pills. David also gives Bowie and Ajax ginger snaps every night around 9:30. When he, or anyone, flashes the open hands sign, they know that is the end of the snack.

Dr. Eldridge said I could take Bowie on short walks but should use a harness rather than a collar. I didn't want to strain his breathing with a long walk. I wasn't about to use the pronged training collar. I had blamed myself that maybe that was what caused the cancer in Casey's neck. David assured me that it wasn't, but I threw that collar in a drawer. I'll never use it again.

Besides, Bowie isn't a big puller on the leash like Casey was. He doesn't get too excited, except when I try to put the harness on him. Then the dance and chopping, the chopping right in my ear, begin.

We also had to shorten our walks because of Bowie's feet. They are splayed out, almost flattened. After walking on the concrete for a little while,

Bowie really slows down and it's apparent that his feet hurt. I believe the monster who had him, who shot him and let another animal attack him, and left him for dead, kept my Bowie in a cage with a raised, wire floor. A floor not meant for dog feet. A floor that made dog toes and pads spread out unnaturally. A floor that could cut dog's feet. Dr. Eldridge agreed.

Another reason I believe this is that Bowie eats lying down. Oh, he does the dinner dance. He walks and hops backwards on his hindlegs, and jumps up and down and sideways until his bowl of food is set down. Of course he's chopping, too. Then he plops down with his front legs around the bowl and eats. I'm certain he had to eat lying down to give his feet some relief. One of his nipples is enlarged, too. I'm guessing it got caught between the wires.

Hell is getting more crowded.

But for all that he's been through, Bowie is a sweetheart. A true lovebug. I call him "Sweetie Pie" or "BoJaynegles."

As the "no dogs on the couch" rule has long since been revoked, Bowie gets up on the couch. He also gets in my chair with me. Every time, and I mean, every time, he hops up in the chair with me, he stands guard. He plants his front feet squarely on my thigh and looks around with the most noble look. He noses me in my eyes or on my nose with his ice-cold nose, and sniffs my forehead. After a few minutes, he sits down on my legs, then lies down facing me. I stroke him and twirl his soft ears in my hands. He whistles softly.

Bowie likes to lay his head on one of my hands while the other hand pets him. He likes to stick his nose in my hand for a gentle nose hug or tuck his nose and part of his head under my arm. When Bowie is sleeping on my lap, if I talk to him or start petting him again, he will flex all four feet. Sometimes he whistles. Other times he lets out a loud groan and then sighs.

He's very affectionate and I wonder who could have been so mean to my dog. When I run my hands over his scarred legs and haunches and imagine how he cried loud enough for Brince to hear him in the woods, it breaks my heart. I can't imagine how much pain Bowie was in when he was thrown away. So I tell Bowie how very much I love him and that no one will ever hurt him again. He will never have to cry in fear and pain and desertion again. Ever.

If Bowie needs to get up, say because someone is in the kitchen and there could be a snack involved, he will return to my lap, repeating the process of standing guard, sniffing, sitting, and lying down. Lather, rinse, repeat, so to speak.

He is perfectly content to put his forelegs in my lap and stand on his hindlegs while I pet him. Of course, his favorite time to do this is when I'm at the computer writing. In the chair with wheels. And we roll all over the room. Then he will lie in the dog bed next to me while I continue to write. When he needs more attention, he will paw me or get back on his hind legs and put his front legs in my lap.

During our cuddle sessions, I've noticed something else about Bowie's spots. Besides the heart-shaped spot, his belly looks like someone took a circle-shaped stamp, pressed it on an ink pad, and repeatedly stamped Bowie's belly. It has many big black spots on it. Some form a line. His belly looks like a Dalmatian's.

Bowie has several areas with swirlies. He has one on his chest, one under each floppy ear, one behind each upper foreleg, one inside each upper foreleg, and one on each hind leg amid the scars on the backs of his thighs.

I've also noticed that the two large black spots on the left side of his back are side-by-side. They look like angel wings. Enough said. A heart and angel wings. God and Casey at work again.

Although Bowie does have loose skin around his neck, he didn't have the large neck roll like Casey did. It must come with age. When Bowie looks down, a big wrinkle on the top of his head furrows down towards his eyes.

It's pretty cute. He also has a roll on his rear end, just above his tail, when he sits down. He always wags his tail when he sits down,

Bowie is smart, too, as I believe all coonhounds are. He learned immediately where the treat jar is. Ajax is a good teacher. Bowie likes to put his left paw on us, especially if we have forgotten to get him a treat or if the treat, or buttered toast, isn't coming fast enough. Or if our hands aren't petting him.

Counter-surfing is a great pleasure for him as well. Again, he's the perfect height.

At Thanksgiving, I ordered three dozen homemade rolls and lemon meringue pie from Gwenneth, a friend with whom I went to high school and is also a dog rescuer. I brought the food home and went to do something. Justin was sitting at the dining room table, editing a video he had made.

When I came back into the living room, Bowie was in his dog bed by the television, furiously chewing on something. Something kind of big. And yellowish-white. I looked closer and discovered that he had gotten some of the rolls off the counter!

I ran into the kitchen. Sure enough, a pan of rolls was perched precariously at the edge of the island. Of this particular pan, six rolls were MIA. Well, they weren't MIA. They were in Bowie's dog bed and gullet. At least we had two-and-a-half dozen more rolls to eat.

He did the same thing with a box of Chick-Fil-A chicken nuggets. I was looking for them, to eat for my lunch, and they had disappeared. Vanished. Pretty soon the mystery was solved. I found the nugget box. The half-eaten nugget box. Not only had my coonhound wolfed down those nuggets, he had tried to hide the evidence by almost eating the box! Now we make sure that *any* food of any kind is shoved to the middle of the island out of Bowie's reach.

He gives to the beast its food...

Psalm 147:9

Toys are a great pleasure for Bowie and furry toys with heads are short-lived. To date, Bowie has decapitated a fox, bear, raccoon, and frog. We still have the bodies. And the heads. Tails are also a casualty. He loves to play tug-of-war, but it is hard to tug on a small portion of a bear head. Every now and then we will find a leg that once belonged to a critter that once also had a head and a tail.

In February 2020, we fostered Juliet, a coal-black Great Dane mix puppy. ARLO had rescued Juliet and her brother, Duke. Actually, they were owner surrenders. Duke had been hit by a car, and the owners couldn't afford the vet bills, so they let ARLO take him. Duke was placed with a foster family, who became foster failures and adopted him.

Juliet was surrendered, as well. My cousin Cammy offered to foster Juliet. Cammy has two little Yorkshire terriers. She and her family thought a larger dog would be fun.

Cammy has cystic fibrosis. She has had two double lung transplants. Any dog she has must be a dog that doesn't shed.

I picked Juliet up in Okemah and brought her to Cammy's house. Juliet fit right in and was immediately spoiled and inundated with countless toys.

And then Cammy's chest began to tighten. It became hard for her to breathe. With a heavy, broken heart, she called me and said she was allergic to Juliet. I picked Juliet up and agreed to foster her until she could be adopted.

Well, Bowie *loved it!* He and Juliet played and played and played. They shredded toys, they played tug-of-war, they ripped the pool robot cover to shreds, and during certain tug-of-war games, Bowie pulled Juliet around in the dog bed.

A few days later I received a text from Jaime, the ARLO President. Juliet had been adopted! She would be traveling to New York in a matter of days. While I wasn't really thrilled to have a puppy around, my heart cracked a little. I was secretly imagining being a foster failure. But the family who

235

adopted Juliet had already adopted a pit bull from ARLO. They were ready to expand their pack.

So, Bowie's little friend, who at five months was almost as tall as he is, left. He missed her and I think he still does. But I know that he does well with other dogs now. There were two other dogs with him when Wendell and Sheila fostered him. I just really don't think much bothers him.

So far anyway. And I'm grateful for that. I don't want my Bowie to remember the awful things that happened to him.

Besides not being bothered by other dogs, Bowie has yet to meet a stranger, or really even be wary of one, in spite of what this dog has been through. He absolutely *loves* going to the vet! And they love having him. Dr. Eldridge told me that Bowie sure does love to be petted.

Casey had long since shredded the sheepskin rugs in the dog house. So, I put our old lounger cushions in the dog house. It was a noble gesture. Turns out, old cushions were a great pleasure for Bowie, too. Not so much lying on them as chewing them to pieces. Our yard looked like it had snowed as he dug out the old cushion from the dog house and chewed it to pieces. I came home in time to watch him demolish one. He was shaking it like there was a demon inside it. Stuffing was flying everywhere. He got a piece of the cushion and took off with it. He was having an absolute blast. And I was enjoying watching him. Never mind that I'd have to pick up all of that stuffing.

Since it was getting colder, we gathered up the new good cushions and put them in large garbage bags and put them in the garage for the winter.

During the spring of 2020 (height of the Covid-19 pandemic) Ian came home from Washington, D.C., to avoid being locked down there alone. We put the new cushions out on the chairs.

I found one old, faded pillow that a squirrel had chewed a hole in, so I tossed it to Bowie. He was thrilled and in a matter of minutes, the pillow was ripped to shreds, and shaken so that the stuffing was everywhere on our patio.

Only recently has he barked at someone ringing the doorbell. But he doesn't go nuts. He couldn't care less about the pool guys or cleaning lady. David's nephew and niece, Andrew and Coco, who attend college in Arkansas spent the night with us as they drove home to Las Vegas for spring break and Covid-19 online classes. Bowie greeted them like they were long-lost friends and slept with Andrew on the pull-out sofa bed.

Bowie does appear to have a little bit of separation anxiety when I leave. It kind of makes me proud, but it was hard in the winter when I couldn't leave them outside. My yoga classes are varied, but most of them are in the morning, and David comes home at lunch so he can let the dogs out. Bowie always barks when I leave. Always.

Once, as I was about to leave, I went to the garage to put something in the back seat of the truck. I left the truck door open because I had to get something else. Bowie followed me into the garage and hopped in the truck. He was ready to go with Mom! He did not want me to leave without him.

Treeing Walker Coonhound: ...they do, however, thrive on consistent and ample attention. (22)

For a while, Bowie took it upon himself to urinate in the house at various times while I was gone. He chewed on the wooden panes in our dining room window and chewed up the boxes of toilet paper and paper towels we got from Amazon. I did salvage most of the rolls and stored them in the closet in the garage, hiding them from David. Several rolls of paper towels and toilet paper had chunks chewed out of them. David told me he thought we had a mouse, so I had to confess to him and convict poor Bowie of the crime.

Having Ian here helped immensely. Besides being here with Bowie and Ajax while I was at work, he edited the manuscript for this book. Thank you, Ian!

Chopping is common with Bowie, too. He chops when I leave. He chops when I'm trying to put his harness on for a walk. He chops when I am getting his supper ready. He chops when I'm filling up my tumbler with water because he knows that I'm leaving. Whenever he starts chopping, he hops a little and his front feet lift off the ground. It is pretty cute.

Bowie bays in the yard. At things seen and unseen. He bays as he patrols the yard, smelling whatever critter dared enter his yard during the night. It appears he just likes to run around and bay, even if there's no scent of a critter to be found.

But I have not yet heard Bowie sing. Ian and Justin asked me if I had tried to get him to sing. No. I'd love for him to sing. But I told them that right now, that is a special thing Casey did for me. In time I'm sure I'll encourage Bowie to sing. And I know that when he does, it will be a beautiful song. And I'll probably cry. Right now, though, I'm content listening to Bowie bark for me when I leave and hearing him whistle. I have many videos on my phone of Casey singing to me that I listen to from time to time.

Fast forward to February, 2021. I have now had my sweet Bowie for almost a year and a half. I am happy to report that his separation anxiety appears to be a thing of the past. When I'm getting ready to leave, and fill up my water bottle, he starts chopping. I give him and Ajax a dental stick and that satisfies him when I leave. If I'm only gone for a short period of time, he and Ajax stay in the house. When I get home, the house is relatively unscathed, with the exception of a dog bed moved here or there. I usually find a pair of my shoes in his dog bed. They are not chewed up, but rather just there. He has a favorite couch pillow, too, (with dogs on it) and occasionally I will come home and find it in his dog bed. It's the pillow I use when I take a nap. If I'm going to be gone for a few hours, they go outside, weather permitting.

Bowie's heartworms are pretty much gone, too! He is able to go on longer walks now; I just have to make sure that his feet don't get too sore. He fits right in with us and makes me laugh a lot.

For the record, Bowie and Ajax were by my side as I wrote the last part of this book. I've also been commissioned to write *The Complete Guide to Treeing Walker Coonhounds* and the dogs are "helping" me write that, too, whether they are curled up beside me or helping me eat my cashews. When Bowie thinks I've worked long enough and he needs some attention, he paws me. I oblige. If I've worked for several hours, we have to take a break and get in the recliner together.

Bowie is developing his coonhound neck roll, too. He's also developing some other "rolls" (I blame it on the prednisone), so he may need to be put on a d-i-e-t.

He absolutely *loves* going to the vet! Bowie knows that when I turn left out of our addition, we are going to the vet. He starts barking and when I turn right onto Memorial Road, he goes nuts! He can't wait to get out of the truck and go see the vet, vet techs, receptionists, and whoever else is there.

Bowie also knows that when we turn right out of the addition, we are going to the groomer. He goes nuts, too! He loves it, plus the fact that he gets a pig-in-a-blanket from the donut shop. I take one to Kristen, my groomer, too, as well as her whippet, Patches. But I have to tear it up for Patches as he won't gobble it up like Bowie does. Ajax prefers a couple of donut holes. I know…diet. It is only every couple of months and I figure Bowie deserves it.

Even though I still have not heard a song from Bowie, he does still whistle, whether he is sleeping on the couch or laying in my lap. He whistled the first time I met him. Perhaps Bowie prefers to whistle instead of sing. Maybe this is his song for me. If this is Bowie's song to me, it is beautiful and I love it. It is enough.

I know the longer that I have Bowie, the more stories I can tell. Maybe that will be for another book. He is a sheer delight, a super sweet goofball, and I truly believe that he is a gift from God and Casey.

Every good thing bestowed and every perfect gift is from above, coming down from the Father of lights, with whom there is no variation, or shifting shadow.

James 1:17

Chapter 17

What Heaven Must Be Like

A couple of days after Casey died, I was sitting in my chair in the living room. I heard a noise come from the study room. It sounded like Casey's tags, like they sounded when he walked from the study room into the living room. I immediately turned my head to look for him. He wasn't there, but I promise you I heard those tags!

I've also had some dreams or visions about Casey. Very real and very vivid.

Some of my favorite photos I took of Casey were when he was standing by our swimming pool. In my first dream, I was outside by our pool. Casey was out there, too, and he was magnificent! His coat was so bright and clean, almost glowing. He was so healthy. And then he hopped in bed with me and laid next to me. I wrapped my arms around him and got to hug my beautiful boy one more time. When I woke up, my arms were wrapped around the place where Casey had been.

The second time I dreamed about him, or saw him, I heard him walking into our bedroom. I woke up, sat up in bed, and he walked up next to me. Again, even in the dark, he was bright and clean and healthy. He was glowing.

I saw Casey again a third time. I woke up and saw a coonhound shadow next to Juliet's crate in our bedroom. I know it wasn't Bowie, because he was asleep in the living room. On the couch.

The last time that I saw Casey, as of the printing of this book, I woke up in the middle of the night. There was a dark shadow of a coonhound sitting in the middle of the bed. I sat up to pet him, knowing it was Casey. And then he was gone.

Some of you who are reading this might think I'm a little crazy. But I saw what I saw. And it was very vivid. And I remember it. Many times, we forget our dreams. But these four instances were very real to me. Whether or not I see Casey in a dream or vision again, or hear his tags, he will always be in my heart. But I think God wanted to let me know that Casey is okay.

We all have our ideas of what Heaven will be like, we just can't truly imagine it. God tells us that. I mentioned it in Chapter 3. But this is my go-to scripture, when I'm sad, when someone I love dies, while I grieve for Casey, and what I send to everyone who loses a pet.

...but just as it is written, "Things which eye has not seen and ear has not heard, and which have not entered the heart of man, all that God has prepared for those who love Him."

I Corinthians 2:9

Next to this highlighted verse in my bible is a reference to another scripture.

And every created thing which is in heaven and on the earth and under the earth and on the sea, and all things in them, I heard saying, "To Him who sits on the throne, and to the Lamb, be blessing and honor and glory and dominion forever and ever."

Revelation 5:13

EVERY creature is praising God! That warms my heart. I know there are religious "scholars" who pooh-pooh the idea that animals are in heaven. And I think that is sad. They are putting God in a box.

It's true that God didn't send Jesus to die for animals, but He also didn't destroy them in the flood. He saved them. He put a lot of thought into creating all of the different types of animals, their habits, their mating rituals and gestations, their migrations, their communication with each other. Why throw that away?

To go even further, God tells us that there are horses in heaven!

And I saw heaven opened; and behold, a white horse, and He who sat upon it is called Faithful and True; ...And the armies which are in heaven, clothed in fine linen, white and clean, were following Him on white horses.

Revelation 19:11,14

So as far as my beliefs go, I truly, truly, truly believe that our pets, and many other animals, are waiting for us in heaven. People who don't believe that are putting limits on God. He is much bigger than that. Even though we absolutely cannot imagine what heaven will be like, it's fun to try. And I will never ever discourage someone from believing that they will see their precious pets again.

My nephew, Travis, lost his beloved German Shepherd, Sassy, a few months after Casey died. He beautifully summed up what it is like to lose a pet, a member of our family.

What can we say when we say goodbye to a beloved pet? To simply say "goodbye" is too little but must thus encompass a future lifetime of thoughts and memories, and equally acknowledge the joyous past. Pets give us the perspective and gift of simplicity: to worry less of the mortgage or the COVID-19 and instead, the desire for just another pat on the head or another treat. They can never understand more than love, for what need does a pet have if they are loved? (Except treats.)

But we must in the end say goodbye.

Perhaps the greatest tragedy is we can never truly explain to a pet what they mean to us. But perhaps the greatest triumph is we never need to.

I, for one, cannot wait to get to heaven. I will get to see Daddy and my grandparents and Leroy and many others who have gone on before me. And I will get to see my pets. They will be there. All of them. And Casey will be at the Pearly Gate, a gate which never closes, singing his song to welcome me Home.

Chapter 18

How You Can Help

If you've never rescued, fostered, or adopted a dog, you can start now. You've already taken a big step by reading this book and learning about the plights of dogs, particularly coonhounds, everywhere.

Fostering allows you to see if the dog is a good fit with you. Even if you're not intent on keeping the dog, you're giving it a chance to live in a real home, to be a dog. To be loved. To be a part of a family. To trust. When that dog is adopted, foster another one.

Support local animal rescue groups. Most of these organizations are dependent entirely upon donations. National organizations have hundreds of thousands of dollars coming in. They have salaried staff as well. Most local rescues are run solely by volunteers. Your money goes farther with local rescues.

Volunteer. Help out at fundraisers, adoption events, tell people about the local rescues.

I went over most of this in Chapter 6. But I have listed several organizations that need your help, service, and donations. Spread the word on Facebook and other social media outlets. I'm pretty sure that whatever breed of dog you're looking for, there's a rescue for that breed. Most local rescues aren't breed specific, but usually we (ARLO) never know what kind of dog we are going to get. It's never boring. It's never predictable.

Check out these sites. Some are coonhound specific. I will gladly provide copies of my book to any of these rescues if they want to sell books to raise much-needed funds for their rescues.

- Animal Rescue League of Okemah, P.O. Box 214, Okemah, Oklahoma 74859 (918) 623-6457 www.arlorescue.org, arlokemah@gmail.com Facebook: Animal Rescue League of Okemah

- Diane's Oklahoma Hound Dog Rescue (Facebook)

- Helpless Hounds Dog Rescue in Tulsa, OK (Facebook) (918) 813-3707 helplesshounds@gmail.com https://www.petfinder.com/member/us/ok/tulsa/ helpless-hounds-dog-rescue-ok491/

- Horse and Hound Rescue (Facebook) 2350 S. Midwest Blvd., Guthrie, Oklahoma 73044 (405)206-4689 http://www.horse-andhoundrescue.com/ info@horseandhoundrescue.com

- All Hounds on Deck (Facebook), allhoundsondeck@gmail.com http://www.AllHoundsOnDeck.com

- Coonhound and Foxhound Companions, Inc. started the Long Ears Alive! veterinary fund to save coonhounds and foxhounds, who are in shelters or pounds, and have non-life-threatening medical issues from being euthanized. They started the Coonhound Rescue Network Page and

Coonhound Companions on Facebook.
http://www.coonhoundcompanions.com/

- Coonhounds Needing Rescue! (Facebook)

- Old Friends Senior Dog Sanctuary (Facebook) 12110 Lebanon Road, Mount Juliet, Tennessee 37122 (615) 754-5617 fb@ ofsds.org https://ofsds.org/

- 3 Girls Animal Rescue, Inc. (Facebook), http://3girlsanimal-rescue.org/

- Gentle Jake's Coonhound Rescue, houndrescue@yahoo.ca http://www.coonhoundrescue.ca/about-us

- Operation Helping Hounds (Facebook) transports and relocates hounds from all over the United States to Priceless Pet Rescue in California. https://www.operationhelpinghounds.org/

- Priceless Pet Rescue (Facebook) (909) 203-3695 https://price-lesspetrescue.org/

Now it's up to you! Thank you for purchasing this book and reading this book. Please rescue a dog. You will probably get rescued, too.

Acknowledgements

First and foremost, as in everything that I do in my life, I must give credit and thanks to God. Without Him, I wouldn't even have a life, much less have the ability to write about parts of it. God is the one who knew me before I was, and wove into my being a deep love for dogs. And it was God who sent Casey and Bowie to me. In fact God sent all of my dogs to me. I believe that He allows, and even desires, for us to meet certain animals, and people as well, at certain times, at appropriate times, to love and to learn.

My family has always supported my love for dogs, even if they might not fully understand just how important dogs, and now rescuing them, are to me. I think special thanks need to be made to David as I have brought home dogs to live with and become part of our family, including my wonderful coonhounds, as well as the dogs I have fostered (and will foster). All of my family has laughed with me about my dogs, loved my dogs, and cried with me as my dogs have gone to heaven.

Along the lines of family, I want to thank Ian for the initial editing of *Rescuing Used Coonhounds*. Valerie proofread this for me as I finished it, providing more sets of eyes to catch misspelled words I might have missed. Justin Jayne and Rachel Lobaugh were on standby to help me navigate the computer to create the book cover and design, but BookBaby made it very easy so I didn't have to enlist their help! It's extremely handy to have a son and sister with English degrees as well as a son who is working on his degree in Creative Digital Media.

Thank you to everyone who has purchased a copy of this book.

I absolutely must thank everyone who has ever rescued or helped rescue a dog, or any kind of animal for that matter. I appreciate the responses from my LWMRC friends for sharing their stories and for saving their coonhounds. For everyone involved in animal rescue, including my friends with ARLO, thank you.

May God bless each and every one of you! May God bless His hounds!

OTHER BOOKS BY ANN M. JAYNE

Kory's Jungle

Eat Like A Local-Oklahoma

50 Things to Know About Teaching Yoga

The Complete Guide to Treeing Walker Coonhounds
(available mid-late 2021 from LP Media)

amjayne@cox.net

Some Hounds in Literature

- *Shiloh, Shiloh Season, Saving Shiloh,* and *A Shiloh Christmas* by Phyllis Reynolds Naylor
- *Sounder* by William H. Armstrong
- *Where the Red Fern Grows* by Wilson Rawls

Some Hounds in Movies

- *A Christmas Story*
- *Overboard* (Kurt Russell!)
- *Shiloh*
- *Sounder*
- *The Aristocats,* Walt Disney Animation
- *The Fox and the Hound,* Walt Disney Animation (Kurt Russell!)
- *Tombstone* (Kurt Russell!)
- *Where the Red Fern Grows*

Some Hounds in Songs

- *Born on the Bayou* by Creedence Clearwater Revival
- *Hound Dog* by Elvis Presley
- *Ol' Red* by Blake Shelton

References

All scripture was taken from the *Master Study Bible*, New American Standard, Holman Bible Publishers, Nashville, Tennessee 37234, 1981.

http://www.animallaw.info/statute

"Cross Timbers," Bruce W. Hoagland, *The Encyclopedia of Oklahoma History and Culture*, https://www.okhistory.org/publications/enc/entry.php?=CR016.

"Key Underwood Coon Dog Memorial Graveyard," http://coondogcemetery.com, 2005.

(1), (2), (3), (6), (7), (8), (10), (13), (14), (15), (18), (19), (20), (21), (22) *The Mini Atlas of Dog Breeds*, James B. Johnson and Andrew De Prisco, T.F.H. Publications, Inc., Neptune City, New Jersey 07753, 1990, pp 274, 283, 285, 289, 294, 328, 334, 350, 412, 458.

(4), (5), (9), (11), (12), (16), (17) *The Complete Dog Breed Book,* First published in the United States as *Top Dog* in 2012, Dorling Kindersley, DK Publishing, New York 10014, 2014, pp. 50, 75, 144, 152, 161, 162.

Merriam-Webster.com Dictionary, Merriam-Webster, https://www.merriam-webster.com/dictionary/rescue.

"History of the English Coonhound," Pete Nicolai,
https://www.uebfa.org/index.php/breed-history
United English Breeders & Fanciers Association, 2020

"History of the July Hound," Rodney Sweat, HuntingDawgs.com,
http://raydelaney.net/dawgs/hd1_july_hound_history.html;
all information taken from *American Foxhunting: An Endangered Sport,*
Sarah Strahan, 1965, 1993, published by Privatly.

"Alabama's Coon Dog Cemetery," Daniel Wallace, https://gardenandgun.com/feature/alabamas-coon-dog-cemetery/ April/May 2014.